IMAGES
of America

PLAINSBORO

To my wife, Andrea, for her love and support and to my parents, William S. Hart and Joan Dougher Hart, for their love and sacrifices.

IMAGES
of America

PLAINSBORO

Bill Hart

ARCADIA
PUBLISHING

Published by Arcadia Publishing
Charleston, South Carolina

Library of Congress Catalog Card Number: 2002115977

For all general information, contact Arcadia Publishing:
Telephone 843-853-2070
Fax 843-853-0044
E-mail sales@arcadiapublishing.com
For customer service and orders:
Toll-free 1-888-313-2665

Visit us on the Internet at www.arcadiapublishing.com.

CONTENTS

ACKNOWLEDGMENTS

My first thanks, as when I wrote *East Orange,* go to my wife, Andrea Alam Hart. Once again, she agreed to be a "research widow" as I spent six months of weekends either at the Plainsboro Museum or locked away in my office. Her love, support, and advice are immeasurable.

A book such as this cannot be written without the aid and encouragement of many people. I endeavor here to thank all of them. It is my fervent hope that I have not left anyone out.

First, I wish to thank Robert Yuell, executive director of the Plainsboro Historical Society. More than anyone else, Robert made this book possible. He gave me access to the museum and made available to me all photographs and files. He painstakingly read every caption, made corrections, and where necessary, did a rewrite. His research over the years was the source of many captions. I also thank his wife, Michele Spelke, another research widow.

Next, thanks go to Matt Hafenmaier of the Plainsboro Historical Society. Matt was tenacious in his efforts to obtain photographs that the museum did not have. His keen memory of people and events was invaluable to the accuracy of the material. Along with Robert, he reviewed every caption. My thanks also go to Lynda Hafenmaier, the third research widow in this story.

Rudy Wellnitz, president of the Plainsboro Historical Society, also deserves thanks. Besides his encouragement, Rudy supplied additional photographs from his own and other sources. Rudy, like Matt, has a keen memory of people and events that was instrumental in putting the material together. Rudy also checked every caption.

Many other people aided me in some way, but unfortunately, space does not allow me to give the details. I hope they will accept my sincere thanks. They include Savanah Jackson Mapelli; Jinny Baeckler, director of the Plainsboro Library; Lt. Elizabeth L. Bondurant, the Plainsboro Police Department; Rev. John G. Nugent, C.M., St. Joseph's Seminary; Rev. Joseph A. Morris, C.M., Superior, St. Joseph's Seminary; Kerry Patzke, senior associate, Burson-Marsteller; Robert B. Young, assistant vice president, Merrill Lynch; David Knights and Diane Vernickas, the Princeton Forrestal Center; John Layendecker, Firmenich; Mike Corey, the American Re-Insurance Company; John Kling, FMC; Beth Reilley, Princeton Alliance Church; Patricia Hullfish, township clerk, Plainsboro Township; Patty Wieser and Elle Starkman, the Princeton Plasma Physics Laboratory; Stephanie Solarski, the Plainsboro Rescue Squad; Bill Toikka, the Plainsboro Historical Society; Evelyn Wicoff, the Plainsboro Historical Society; Priscilla Stitt, the Plainsboro Historical Society; Steven Schneider; and Emily Ruedemann Gorgianni.

I wish also to thank my editor, Susie Jaggard, for all of her support and for putting up with my numerous questions.

Finally, my thanks go to the members of the Plainsboro Historical Society. The research they conducted over the years made my job much easier. I also extend my gratitude to Mayor Peter Cantu and the Plainsboro Township Committee for their continuing support of the Plainsboro Historical Society.

INTRODUCTION

I grew up in East Orange, a suburb of Newark and a sizeable city on its own. It was a beautiful town, with large homes, luxurious apartment buildings, and unparalleled shopping. (A few years ago, I was lucky enough to capture that city's rich history in a book for Arcadia Publishing.) When I married, I left East Orange, and my wife, Andrea, and I made our first home in Belleville, where we lived for several years. Eventually, we decided to leave the hustle and bustle of northern New Jersey behind us and move to central New Jersey. That part of the state was still largely undeveloped and primarily farmland. That suited us fine.

The town we moved to in 1984 was called Plainsboro. I had never heard of it. All I knew was that it was near Princeton. In fact, the development into which I was moving had a Princeton address. This added to my confusion and to that of my family and friends. When I told them I had moved to Plainsboro, I would get a blank stare in response, followed by a "Where?" I soon learned it was much easier to say that I lived in Princeton and leave it at that.

Plainsboro was a town in flux at that time. Only 20 years before, there had not been a development in it. By the mid- to late 1980s, it was the fastest-growing town in New Jersey; the population had more than tripled and was rising rapidly. I watched as farm after farm was dug up and developments took their place. Huge industrial parks were being built. I watched sadly as the immense Walker-Gordon silos were torn down, signifying the final footnote to that institution's storied life as a dairy farm.

Throughout these years, I was unaware of the rich history of Plainsboro. I spent far more time in Princeton. It was in Princeton that I generally dined, shopped, or went for an evening drive. In this regard, I was like many others. Plainsboro, like many of the surrounding towns, lies in the shadow of her big sister to the southwest. This does not, however, take anything away from that lovely, quaint town. Princeton is steeped in history. The university there is one of the leading colleges in the country, and the research and philanthropic endeavors conducted by them have helped to aid countless lives.

Admittedly, it would sometimes be frustrating to read an article about a research facility at the Forrestal campus in Plainsboro and never once see that town's name mentioned. Instead, the reporter would write "Such-and-Such Company" of Princeton or would simply refer to the location as an area "north of Princeton." It was as if Plainsboro did not exist.

My own admission into the secret history of Plainsboro occurred slowly. It happened when I began to write historical articles for the now defunct *West Windsor–Plainsboro News Eagle* in 1998. Gradually I learned things of which I was only vaguely aware. For instance, I had not known that the first Elsie the Cow had lived, died, and was buried in Plainsboro. I did not know of the importance of the Walker-Gordon Dairy to the milk industry on a national level. I was unaware of the extensive research conducted at the Forrestal campus and surrounding area that included fission, fusion, and hovercraft research facilities.

Much of that knowledge did not come until I began to write this book. I was tentative about that opportunity when it came. I could not imagine that there existed the necessary 200 photographs to write an Arcadia book on Plainsboro. However, when I met with Robert Yuell, executive director of the Plainsboro Historical Society, he proved to me that there were that many and more.

I was extremely fortunate in that regard. In the 1970s, local residents, sensing the change their town was about to make, began to do their best to preserve its history. The Plainsboro Historical Society was formed in March 1975. Members of the society worked tirelessly to save buildings, preserve artifacts, take pictures, and collect what photographs, documents, and blueprints existed. The efforts of the society's members paid off, resulting in the Plainsboro Museum. Located in the old Wicoff house on Plainsboro Road, this treasure-filled building is a living testimony to the lives and events of the town of Plainsboro.

Plainsboro is a pictorial history. I have endeavored in this book, wherever possible, to let the photographs speak for themselves and to use the captions only to tell the story that the pictures cannot. Primarily, the book contains photographs, but many postcards are also contained within. Unless otherwise noted, the photographs and postcards are from the collection of the Plainsboro Historical Society. I have attempted to credit all photographs with the donor's name wherever possible, even if that donation happened many years ago. I apologize in advance if I have inadvertently omitted someone. During the writing of this book, many people and companies became aware of the project and reached out to the society to donate pictures. I have used as many of those photographs as possible.

Unfortunately, in every book of this type, some scenes must be left out. This occurs either because no photograph was available, the photograph quality was not good enough to duplicate, or because there was insufficient data to caption the picture. Finally, there are physical limitations. Not every picture could be included. Making those decisions was very difficult.

Primarily, this is a book of what was, not what is. Therefore, I have not always indicated if the building is still standing or what is there today. When a date could be estimated and space permitted, I provided it. Because so much of Plainsboro's history is recent, I elected to include a few photographs from recent years. However, the majority of the photographs are from the period between 1900 and 1970, when large-scale development began.

As noted in the acknowledgments, many people aided me in this endeavor. However, if there are any errors in the book, they are mine, not theirs.

Like *East Orange*, *Plainsboro* was a labor of love. I truly do love my new hometown. In a few more years, I will have lived here longer than I have lived anywhere else. While much has changed, successful efforts have been made to preserve open space. Finding working farms is difficult, but they are there, and a short ride to the outskirts of town can still bring you back in time.

The photographs within this book are a bit of Americana, a look back at a lost era. I hope I have captured the spirit and drive and love of the people who founded and built Plainsboro. I sincerely hope that you enjoy reading *Plainsboro* as much as I enjoyed writing it.

One

HISTORY

As in so many of the cities and towns of New Jersey, the Europeans were not the first humans to live in Plainsboro. In 1982, an archeological dig at the intersection of Scudders Mill Road and Route 1 was conducted. The artifacts found there date back 3,700 years. The archeologists discovered 25,000 items and also "post molds." These post molds indicated the presence of five 15- by 25-foot buildings. Their presence implies a permanent or semipermanent residence. These people, known as the Terminal Archaic Indians, were gatherers of wild plants, nuts, and berries. They also fished and hunted with spears. The use of pots made from soapstone had also started.

Many years later, the land that would become Plainsboro was occupied by the Lenape. The Lenape, which means "Ordinary People," were in their Late Woodland period when the Europeans arrived. They had developed the bow and arrow for hunting but still fished and gathered foodstuffs. In addition, they had developed agricultural methods and grew corn, beans, squash, and other foodstuffs. They lived in a region until the firewood and food supply were exhausted and then moved on, often traveling along rivers such as the Millstone in dugout canoes. The Lenape who lived in Plainsboro may have been part of the Sankhican tribe. They were known to live near Trenton and spoke the Unami dialect. Their land was called Lenapehoking (the land of the Lenape), and they were a peaceful people.

The arrival of the Dutch in New Jersey in the 17th century marked the end of the Lenape way of life. The Dutch first formed colonies in Fort Nassau (Glouster City) in 1624 and Pavonia (Jersey City) in 1630. The Swedes also built settlements on the Delaware River, but these were taken over by the Dutch in 1655. By 1664, the Dutch were defeated by the English. James, the brother of King Charles II of England, divided the land between the Hudson and Delaware Rivers between his friends Sir George Carteret and Lord Berkeley. They called the colony New Jersey. Berkeley controlled the southwestern half, called West Jersey, and Carteret controlled the rest, called East Jersey. The future town of Plainsboro was located in East Jersey. In 1682, the county of Middlesex was formed, but it was 20 more years before the east and west colonies were united to form the Royal Province of New Jersey.

The date of the first European settlement in Plainsboro is not known. However, Cranbury was settled in 1697. Settlers may even have lived there as early as 1680. The presumed oldest structure in Plainsboro, which is still standing, is located at 4 Dey Road, near the intersection of Plainsboro Road. This building was an early tavern, called an "ordinary." It dates back to at least the early 1700s and possibly the 1680s. If this can ever be established, the building would prove to be the oldest surviving ordinary in America. This ordinary may have been part of an early settlement made by one Josiah Pricket, a butcher from Burlington in West Jersey. The small settlement, built in the 1680s, was to have been located on "Cranberry Brook" west of the town of Cranbury.

The earliest settlements in Plainsboro were farms. The land was fertile and water was readily available from several ponds and brooks. Devil's Brook, Cranbury Brook, and the Millstone River were the major waterways. This water also served as a power source, and mills sprang up to grind grain and saw wood. Although Plainsboro proper was located at the intersection of Plainsboro and Dey Roads, where the ordinary was located, different regions of the village took on a life of their own. These developed their own names, such as Aqueduct, Mapleton, and Scotts Corner.

An 1861 map of South Brunswick shows the village of Plainsboro. South Brunswick Township, founded in 1798, held all of the lands that would become Plainsboro Township until 1872. In that year, the lands south of Plainsboro Road and Dey Road was given to the newly formed Cranbury Township. The map provides us with the names of some of the early residents, such as Van Dyke, Grover, Davison, Perrine, Wyckoff, Dye, and Britton.

Exactly how Plainsboro acquired its name is unknown. One theory is that the ordinary was known as the Plane Tavern, leading to the name Plainsborough. Another story says the region was called the "Borough of the Plains" or simply "the Plains." A document from 1760 refers to the "Tract of Land situated in Cranberry Plains between Cranberry Brook and Devils Brook." In 1848, a post office was established and was called "Plainsborough." This was shortened in 1894 to "Plainsboro" by presidential decree, and the name remained unchanged.

Local farmers had numerous ways to send their cash crops to market and receive seed, farm implements, and other sundries. These included the Trenton and New Brunswick Turnpike (Route 1), which was chartered in 1804 for 99 years; the Delaware and Raritan Canal, which was completed in 1834; the Camden and Amboy Railroad, which was opened in 1839; and the trolley line, which connected Trenton and New Brunswick in 1902.

In 1918, the superintendent of public education for Middlesex County reviewed the schools in the village of Plainsboro. He was concerned that some of the schoolchildren were being taught on the second floor of a wood-frame building with only one stairway. This was the Grange Hall. He decreed that a new school must be built. Since this portion of Plainsboro was in the Cranbury School District, local citizens appealed to them for relief. Cranbury declined. As a result, several prominent citizens petitioned the New Jersey legislature to form a new town. The petition was granted, and on May 6, 1919, Plainsboro Township was founded. From this development came the "Princeton Stone" four-room school, now known as the Wicoff School.

Plainsboro continued as a farm town for most of the 20th century. In 1897, the Walker-Gordon Dairy began purchasing land in Plainsboro. Soon Walker-Gordon was the town's largest employer and purchaser of farm crops. Most of the other major farms raised potatoes, wheat, and corn. The standing joke was that Plainsboro had more cows than people, and until the second half of the 20th century, this was true. In 1916, the Rockefeller Institute for Medical Research came to Plainsboro and thereby began Plainsboro's long history as a research area. By the early 1970s, however, change was coming. Farmers began to sell their land to developers. Where once grew crops of potatoes, corn, and alfalfa, houses and condominiums now sprang from the earth. In 1971, Walker-Gordon ceased dairy operations. It was replaced over the years by such corporate giants as Firmenich, FMC (Food Machinery and Chemical Corporation), the American Re-Insurance Company, Merrill Lynch, and Bristol-Myers Squibb. In the 1980s, Plainsboro was the fastest-growing town in New Jersey. Today, it is home to more than 20,000 people.

The little farm town is all grown up.

This 1861 map of South Brunswick shows the region that became Plainsboro Township. A close look at the map under the large word "Plainsboro" shows a "Store and P.O." located in the third building west of Dey Road on the north side of Plainsboro Road. Just to the left of the capital letter *P*, the word "school" appears. On the east side of Dey Road and the north side of Plainsboro Road, you can see the "J. Hutchinson Hotel." West of the hotel is a blacksmith shop and a wheelwright shop, with a second wheelwright shop across the street. Farther west (left) on Plainsboro Road, the map shows the location of Plainsboro's Methodist Episcopal church. Toward the end of Maple Avenue, to the left of the pond, you can see the name "R. Stockton" and a "Grist and Saw Mill" that he owned. To the far left, at the intersection of Route 1 and Plainsboro Road, the blacksmith shop is marked as "BS shop." The names Williamson and Scudder also appear there. Just off Route 1 is the word "school," indicating the probable location of the Mapleton School. In the Aqueduct area, the Van Dykes owned most of the land that later became St. Joseph's Seminary, Princeton Landing, Princeton Forrestal Village, Princeton Nurseries, and the Princeton Forrestal campus. In the center of the map, the name Britton appears repeatedly, the Brittons being one of the earliest families and largest landowners in town. Moving a little to the east (right), the word "school" appears again at the intersection of Dey and Scotts Corner Roads.

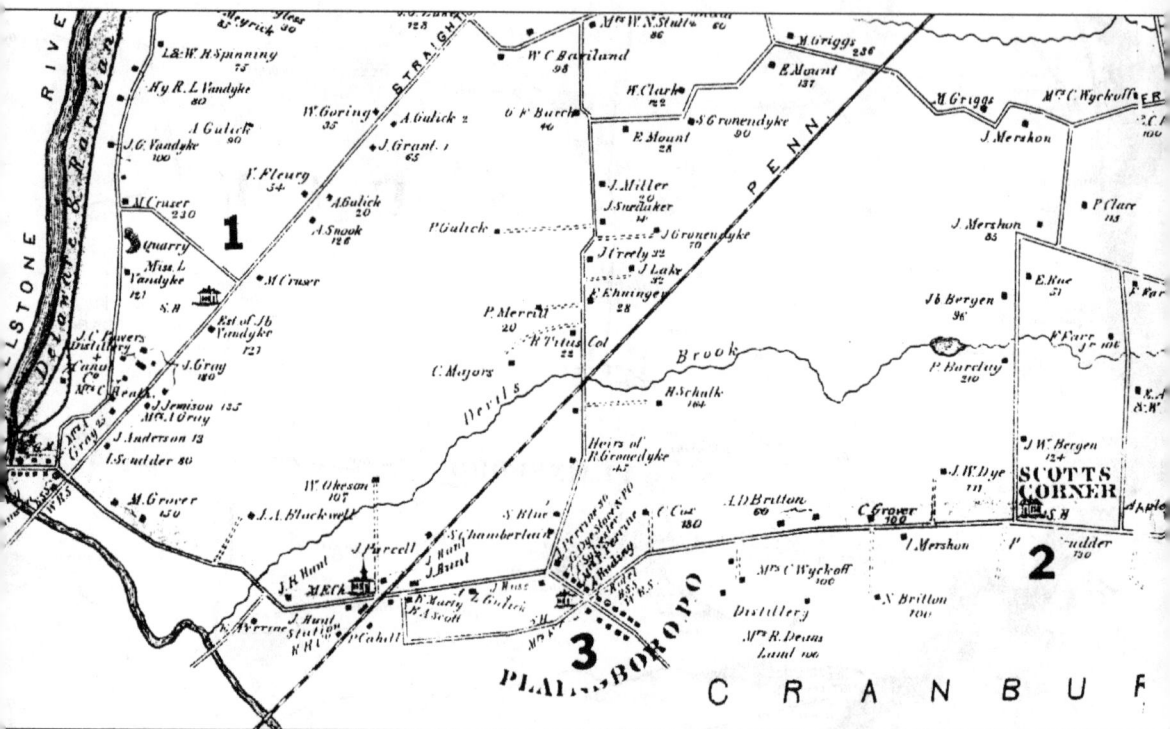

This map of South Brunswick Township was created in 1876 by Everetts and Stewart of Philadelphia. The biggest change in 15 years shown on this centennial map is that the Pennsylvania Railroad has built a line through the center of town, and the village of Plainsboro has been "split" between South Brunswick and Cranbury. The train station can be seen to the lower left, just below the drawing of the Methodist Episcopal church. On the left side of the map, the present-day Route 1 is now clearly marked as the "Straight Turnpike." To the left of the highway, many of the same names continue to appear, although now they are accompanied by numbers, presumably the acreage owned. The region where the Van Dykes lived is indicated on some maps as "Mapleton." The road that later became Sayre Drive connects the Straight Turnpike and Mapleton Road. In the Aqueduct section (extreme lower left), the blacksmith shop is accompanied by a wheelwright shop and a nearby store. In town, the post office is indicated as "G. Dye Store and P.O." A school is shown near its present location on Plainsboro Road. Moving north along Schalks Crossing Road, the map shows the farms of C. Majors and R. Titus. Titus was the name of the first black family in town, and the family's founder was a runaway slave. The Gronendyke (Groendyke) farm also appears. In the lower center part of the map is Scotts Corner, where a school is indicated. Like Aqueduct and Mapleton, Scotts Corner appears to be considered almost a separate village.

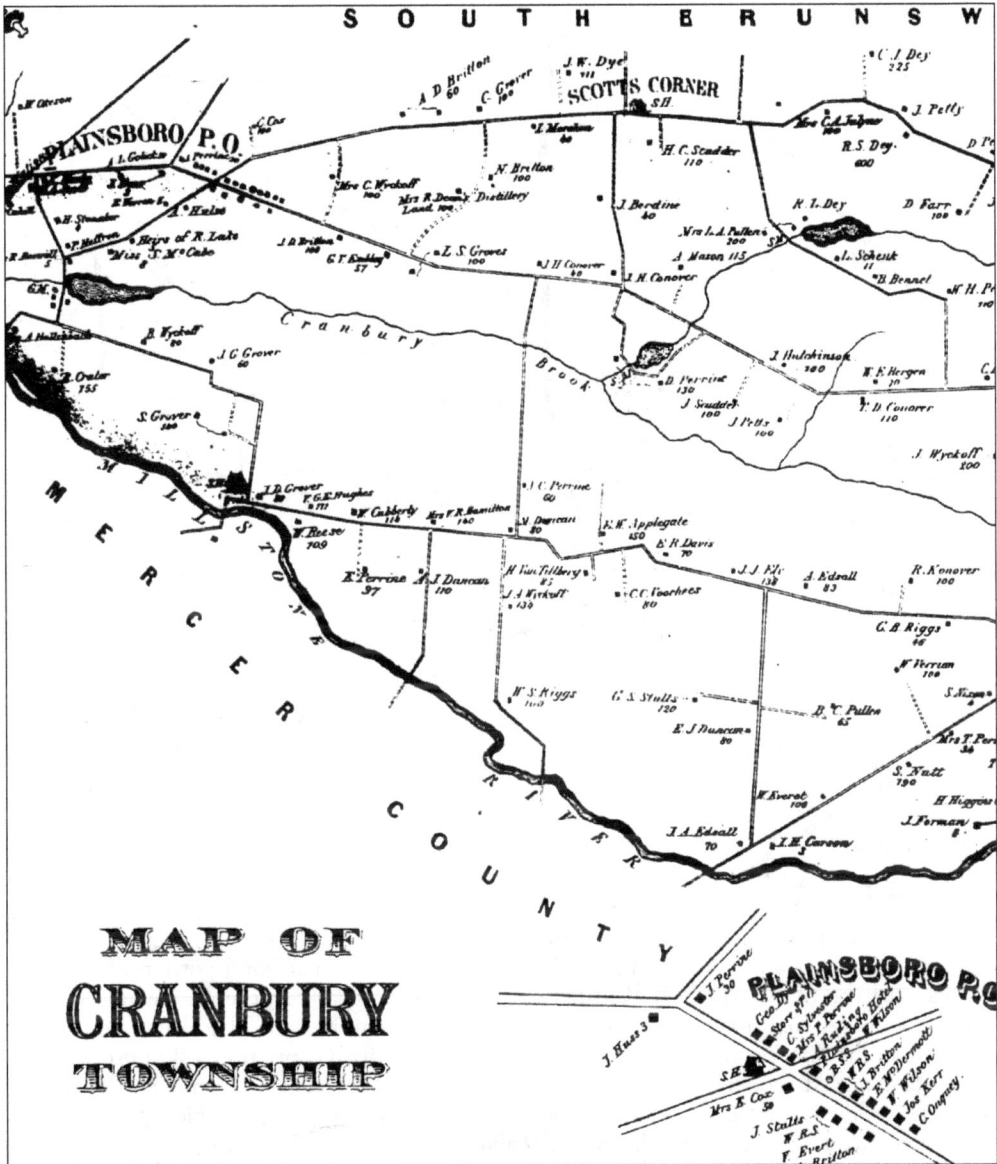

Another Everetts and Stewart map shows Cranbury Township as it appeared in 1876. The small "blown-up" portion of Plainsboro gives a clear view of the location of the post office, school, hotel, and shops. Notice that the "Store & P. O." is located in the same building as in the map from 1861. Also note that the blacksmith shop is owned by W. Wilson. It appears in this section that J. Britton owns the wheelwright shop on the north side of Plainsboro Road, and J. Stults owns the one across the street. A school is indicated on the southwest corner of Plainsboro and Dey Roads. On the main map, to the right of the phrase "Plainsboro P.O.," we see the name "Mrs. C. Wyckoff" (Catherine Lucretia Britton Wicoff). She was a daughter of Col. Dean Britton and Mary Dye Britton. Dean Britton died without a will on June 18, 1870, and this property was sold to Catherine from the estate in 1872. This became the Wicoff farm. The J.D. Britton farm appears on Plainsboro Road, where today's Gospel Fellowship Church is located.

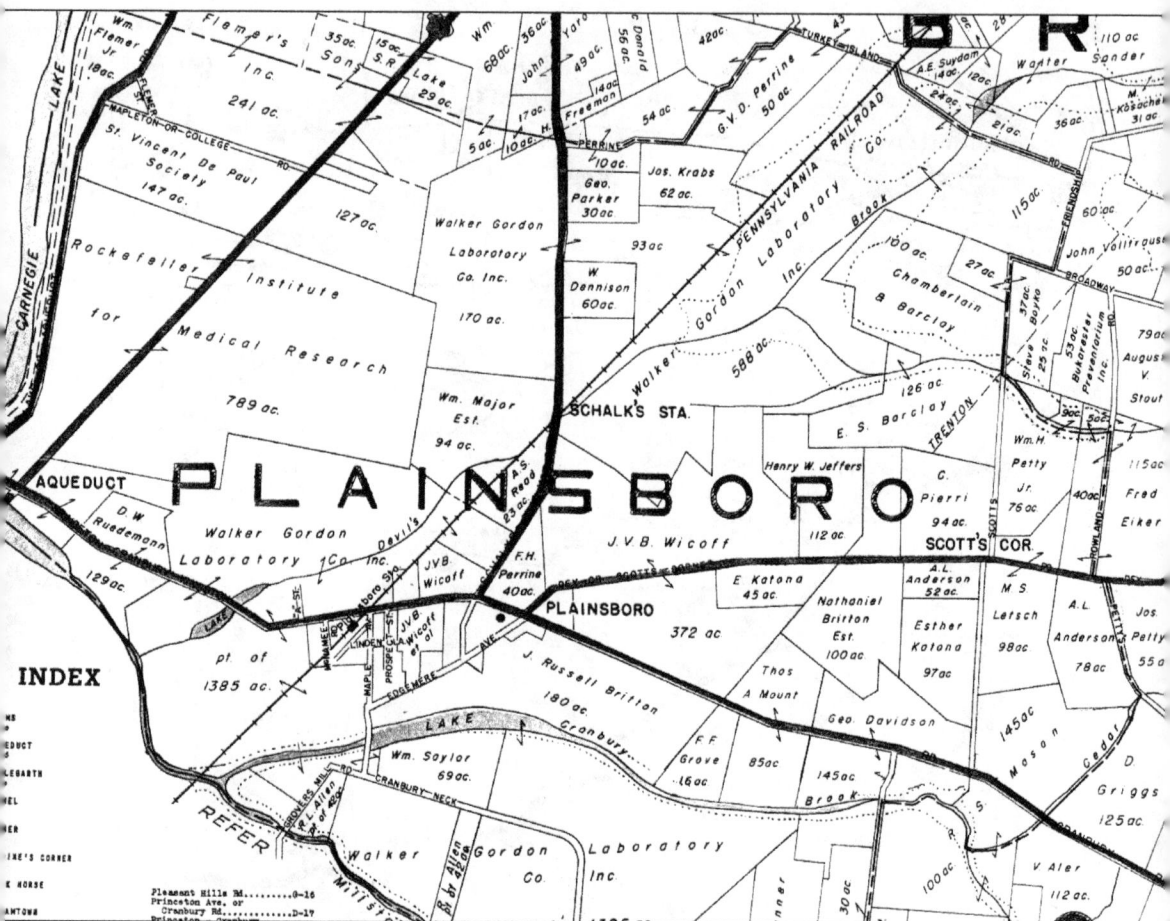

In this 1939 map, Plainsboro appears much as it was for the first three quarters of the 20th century. The farms and acreage are all clearly marked. In the left-hand portion of the map, you can see the St. Vincent De Paul Society, better known as St. Joseph's Seminary or St. Joseph's College. Next to the seminary is the land of William Flemer. The Flemer home dates from before the American Revolution. A shot fired by a British cannon in a skirmish with the colonists damaged the exterior of the home. The damage can still be seen. The Rockefeller Institute for Medical Research owns 789 acres of land, where it conducted biological research. Plainsboro Road is called the Princeton-Cranbury-Kingston Road. Moving down Plainsboro Road, from west to east (left to right), you can see the extensive holdings of the Walker-Gordon Laboratory. The Plainsboro railroad station is still in use. Farther to the right appear several land holdings of "J.V.B Wicoff" and "J. Russell Britton." To the east of that appear the farms of George Davidson (Davison) and R.S. Mason. On Dey Road appear the farms of Henry W. Jeffers Jr. and C. Pierri. On Schalks Crossing Road, you can see the farms of William Major, W. Dennison, and George Parker. On Scotts Corner Road are the E.S. Barclay and William H. Petty Jr. farms. Many of these names appear later in this book.

Two

EARLY SCENES

AND FOUNDERS

The farmers of Plainsboro needed mills to cut their lumber and to grind their grain. Fortunately, the region that made up Plainsboro was supplied with several streams that could be used for power. The Millstone River, Devil's Brook, Shallow Brook, Cedar Brook, and Cranbury Brook all cut across town. This c. 1910 postcard view shows the Plainsboro Mills, which was located on the Cranbury Brook at the dam site on Maple Avenue, near the Plainsboro Pond. Both a gristmill and sawmill stood here. Built before the American Revolution, the mills were damaged during that conflict. A sales advertisement from 1779 describes "100 acres of good land, with a small house and orchard, grist mill and saw mill." This mill was also called Stockton's Mills and Walker-Gordon Mills, the latter being its last owner. The mills were torn down in 1930. This view is on Maple Avenue, looking north toward Plainsboro Pond. The two houses in the background (center, right) are on Edgemere Avenue. Note the bicycle in front of the building, apparently used by a worker to commute. (Courtesy of Evelyn Wicoff.)

Scudder's Mills was located on the Millstone River, not far from the intersection of Mapleton Road and Route 1. The gristmill, sawmill, fulling mill, and carding mill were built by Josiah Davison in 1737. It was later purchased by William Scudder. Left to his son William, a lieutenant colonel in the American army, the mills and Scudder's house were burned by British soldiers in December 1776. The mills were later rebuilt. Over the years, they were known as Gray's Mills and Aqueduct Mills. They were torn down in 1906 for Carnegie Lake.

The area near the intersection of Mapleton Road and Route 1 was called the Aqueduct. The name came from the aqueduct built to carry the Delaware and Raritan Canal over the Millstone River. Mills, storehouses, homes, and other businesses were located there. This photograph is believed to be of the road that once connected Harrison Street to Mapleton Road across the meadows. The road is now buried under the Millstone River basin. (Collection of the Historical Society of Princeton.)

After Scudder, the Aqueduct mills were owned by a Dr. Hunt and later still by Alexander Gray. The mills benefited from the construction of the Delaware and Raritan Canal in 1834, the coming of the Camden Amboy Railroad in 1839, and the proximity to the Straight Turnpike (Route 1) in 1804. The mills stopped operation c. 1900. These unidentified men are sitting on grain sacks that read, "Aqueduct GEM A. Thompson & Co." The photograph is dated October 21, 1889.

A general store, blacksmith shop, and wheelwright shop operated in the Aqueduct region. The wheelwright shop occupied the frame building, and the blacksmith occupied the brick building. They were located on the corner of Mapleton Road and Route 1. This photograph, taken c. 1927, shows the building when it housed a garage. The buildings were torn down shortly thereafter to widen Route 1. Note the sign for Route 26, the old designee of Route 1. (Courtesy of Esther Engelke.)

This 1910 postcard view of the Plainsboro Hotel looks east (to the right) down Plainsboro Road. A tavern may have been built near this spot by Josiah Pricket as early as the 1680s. Lodging for travelers in some form has certainly stood here at the intersection of Dey and Plainsboro Roads since the early 1700s. A section of this building may date back to that time. The tavern is known to have served as a stagecoach stop. The sign says, "Plainsboro Hotel A. MacNamee Prop." (Courtesy of Robert Yuell.)

Dating from c. 1910, this postcard view also looks east down Plainsboro Road. Dey Road and the Plainsboro Hotel are off to the left. Edgemere Road is on the right. The hotel probably housed a tavern through the late 1800s. There are Plainsboro MacNamee beer bottle artifacts that establish this. One source says that a general store was opened c. 1900 in the front portion of the hotel. Frank MacNamee sold the hotel in 1921 to George Bobko. (Courtesy of Robert Yuell.)

Looking east down Plainsboro Road from just below Schalks Crossing Road, this postcard view was taken c. 1910. On the right, the closest building is the two-room schoolhouse, followed by the Grange Hall, followed by J.D. Van Doren's General Store. On the left, the first house is the F.H. Perrine home, later owned by Dr. Guy Dean Jr., Plainsboro's first resident doctor. He lived there from the 1920s to the 1960s.

This view looks west on Plainsboro Road from the intersection of Parkway Avenue and Schalks Crossing Road. The building on the left is believed to be the original manse of the First Presbyterian Church. It was later moved farther west on Plainsboro Road, and the lot now serves as a church parking area. The postcard is postmarked August 30, 1912. (Courtesy of Robert Yuell.)

Taken just west of the entrance to the Fox Run development, this c. 1910 postcard view also looks west on Plainsboro Road. The first home on the left, now demolished, was once that of Napoleon and Bessie Jackson. The second building on the left served as the post office from c. 1900 until 1963. The first home on the right is that of a Mrs. Lattle (1861) and later a "C. Onquey" (1876). The next house west is that of Isaac Barlow.

The house on the right is identified as the "Jolly House." The view looks west, just before the railroad "high" bridge, and was taken from what is today the area in front of the Plainsboro Volunteer Fire Company. This bridge was built c. 1900. Before that, this was a grade crossing. The bridge was raised three feet in 1933, when the line was electrified. The house has been demolished since the 1930s. (Courtesy of Evelyn Wicoff.)

The John V.B. Wicoff House was built *c.* 1880 by John Wicoff and Catherine Lucretia Britton Wicoff. John and Catherine were married on February 3, 1875. They had one child, John Van Buren Wicoff, born on June 9, 1878. John Wicoff died in 1892. The house was modified several times; wings were added in 1893, 1907, and 1928. Pictured here are, from left to right, an unidentified friend, Catherine Lucretia Britton Wicoff, and John Van Buren Wicoff (holding the horse).

John Van Buren Wicoff graduated from Princeton University in 1900 and from New York Law School in 1903. He worked as an attorney out of Trenton. On June 8, 1904, he married Lavinia Ely Applegate. In 1907, they moved into the family home with Catherine, who died in 1928. John worked as a lawyer and banker but also managed the family farm. Pictured *c.* 1904 are, from left to right, an unidentified woman and Lavinia and John Van Buren Wicoff. (Courtesy of Evelyn Wicoff.)

The Wicoffs had seven children. This family photograph was taken in 1922. From left to right are the following: (front row, sitting) Catherine Lucretia Britton Wicoff (John's mother), Marjorie, Evelyn, and Lavinia A. Wicoff (John's wife); (back row, standing) Douglas, John Van Buren, Dorothy, John E., and Catherine Wicoff. The youngest child had not been born yet. (Courtesy of Evelyn Wicoff.)

John Van Buren Wicoff became active in politics in 1908, when he was elected to the Cranbury Township Committee (1908–1919). He was a member of the Cranbury Township Board of Education from 1908 to 1919 and served as president of the Plainsboro Board of Education from that point on. In 1922, he was elected to the Plainsboro Township Committee and was appointed mayor, a position he held until his death. He also served as township attorney. Wicoff died on February 25, 1952.

Pictured here are Henry Jeffers Sr. (left) and John Van Buren Wicoff. Wicoff's greatest contribution to Plainsboro was his role in founding the town. In 1918, the people of Plainsboro urged the Cranbury School Board to build a new schoolhouse in Plainsboro. At that time, the only Plainsboro school available was a two-room schoolhouse built in 1908. The overflow of children was schooled on the second floor of the Grange Hall. The Cranbury School Board declined to build a new school, stating that it would be "unpatriotic" to begin such an undertaking while the war was ongoing. World War I or not, Wicoff and others knew the need was dire. Together with Henry W. Jeffers Sr., P.A. MacNamee, G.B. Philips, Abel H. Updike, and Harry A. Stults, Wicoff and these concerned citizens petitioned the New Jersey state legislature to create a new township called Plainsboro. On February 3, 1919, a bill was introduced to incorporate the township of Plainsboro. The legislation was approved on April 1, 1919, and on May 6, 1919, a mandatory public referendum election was held. There were only two dissenting votes. Plainsboro Township was thereby founded. On May 29, the men mentioned above met to form a new township government and adopted the Declaration of Purposes and Constitution. Henry Jeffers Sr. was elected the first mayor. Seen here in front of the huge Walker-Gordon silos, Henry Jeffers Sr. was born on January 4, 1871, and grew up on a farm in Kingsley, Pennsylvania. Each day, he milked and took care of 20 cows before breakfast. After working on the farm all day, he would once again milk and feed the cows before retiring. It became a lifelong dream of his to make that toil easier. Jeffers went on to study and graduate from Cornell University's first agricultural class in 1898. That same year, he came to work for the Walker-Gordon Laboratory Company in Plainsboro as the farm's manager. In 1919, he became the company's president, a post he held until 1942, at which time he was succeeded by his son Henry W. Jeffers Jr. Jeffers then became chairman of the board, a position he held until his death in 1953. Jeffers was also a director of the First National Bank of Princeton from 1909 to 1953. In 1899, he married Anna C. Adams. Together they had three children. (Courtesy of the Jeffers family.)

23

Jeffers took a scientific approach to dairy farming. He was the inventor of the Rotolactor, a type of merry-go-round for cows that allowed for assembly-line milking. He also held patents for the Jeffers Calculator (a method for measuring a cow's nutritional feeding requirements) and the Jeffers Bacteria Counter (used to count bacterial colonies in a petri dish). Jeffers is shown here at his farm in Kingsley, Pennsylvania, in the late 1940s.

Henry Jeffers Sr. lived and raised his family in Plainsboro. Members of his family are shown here seated on the front steps of the Jeffers house. From left to right are the following: (front row) Henry W. Jeffers Sr., Emily Jeffers Ruedemann, Henry Jeffers Jr., Louise Jeffers Hagenbuch, and Anna Adams Jeffers; (back row) Dana W. Ruedemann and John B. Hagenbuch Jr. From 1942 to 1974, Henry W. Jeffers Jr. served as president of Walker-Gordon. He became mayor of Plainsboro in 1948 and served for 26 years.

The Jeffers house, located on Plainsboro Road, was built between 1919 and 1923. Jeffers allowed his wife, Anna, to do anything she wanted with the house, except for the basement. He declared that to be his. He lined an entire room in the basement with cedar logs and had a huge fireplace built. He also built a small bar. Jeffers did much of his important business and political dealings in that basement. (Courtesy of the Ruedemann family.)

Pictured c. 1930 are Harry A. Stults (left) and Isaac Barlow Jr. Stults worked at Walker-Gordon for 39 years as purchasing agent and treasurer. Stults was instrumental in working out the initial financing of Plainsboro. He was secretary of the Plainsboro Board of Education from 1919 to 1950. He also served as superintendent of Sunday school and was financial secretary of the Plainsboro Presbyterian Church for many years. He died on December 29, 1950. Isaac Barlow Jr. owned the John Deere dealership in town.

The original town founders were, of course, Native Americans. This photograph shows a 1982 archeological dig conducted near the intersection of Route 1 and Scudders Mill Road. The archeologists found 25,000 items, dating back 3,700 years. They also found evidence of five 15- by 25-foot buildings constructed by Lenape ancestors. Route 1 is visible in the background. The building in the upper left is the Hawke house, since demolished.

This photograph shows the archeologists digging down about two feet in five-foot square areas. The debris would then be sifted for artifacts. Most of the items were found in the first three feet of digging. All of the 25,000 items, except for 65 on loan in the Plainsboro Museum, are in the state museum in Trenton.

Three

TRANSPORTATION

The success of an agricultural community is based not only on fertile soil but also on its access to market. In that sense, Plainsboro was ideally located. Halfway between New York and Philadelphia, it was serviced by the Delaware and Raritan Canal, the Pennsylvania Railroad, Route 1, and a trolley line. In 1864, the Camden and Amboy Railroad built a double-track line through Plainsboro. Three years later, the Camden and Amboy Railroad merged with the New Jersey Railroad. This, in turn, became part of the Pennsylvania Railroad in December 1871. In 1873, a third set of tracks was added to the line. Plainsboro is shown as a station stop on an 1874 railroad map. Plainsboro had both a northbound and southbound train station. Shown c. 1905 is the larger of the two, the southbound station, which was then made of wood. (Courtesy of Evelyn Wicoff.)

This c. 1910 postcard view looks north along the railroad tracks. Farther north, railroad maps as old as 1881 show a second stop in Plainsboro called Schalks Crossing. Hermann and Caroline Schalk were wealthy brewers from Newark who, in 1871, built a summer and weekend home (since burned down) in Plainsboro. The stop ceased to be listed in 1914, but the grade crossing remained until a bridge was built in 1948. The steps and pole seen on the extreme left were for the mailbag pickup. (Courtesy of Robert Yuell.)

Before the line was electrified in 1933, steam engines were used. These engines required copious amounts of water. To avoid water stops, track pans (shown in this photograph) were placed inside the tracks. A retractable scoop under the tender brought water up to the water tank as the train moved forward. Plainsboro's pans were located north of the Millstone River. These were a quarter-mile long and six inches deep. Prior to this, standpipe tanks were located at the same spot. Note the hay curing under tarps in the fields. (Courtesy of Oliver Sayler.)

The brick station, built in 1918–1919, was torn down in 1968. Plainsboro service had terminated a few years before. This is a photograph of Wendell Willkie at the station in 1940, when he visited Plainsboro while on a presidential campaign tour. The railroad maintained a labor camp in Plainsboro just north of the Plainsboro Road bridge on the west side of the tracks. During World War II, it was staffed with workers from Mexico. (Courtesy of Evelyn Wicoff.)

This c. 1880s photograph of men unloading boxcars is believed to have been taken in Plainsboro. The man in the white hat (right of center) is William Petty Sr., a Plainsboro farm owner. Besides freight, local mail was also picked up and delivered by train. Figure-eight-shaped mailbags were hung on special posts. As the train rode by, a canelike device snagged the bag and pulled it into the mailcar. Meanwhile, the incoming mail sack was tossed out. (Courtesy of Dorothy Petty Dey.)

The Trenton and New Brunswick "Fast Line" trolley was completed in November 1902. Between 1902 and 1937, the trolley stopped at Cranbury (now Grovers Mill), Plainsboro, and Dey Roads. This c. 1914 postcard photograph looks west on Plainsboro Road, from about where the traffic light entrance to Princeton Meadows Shopping Center is today. This station was completed on October 29, 1903. Trolley cars also delivered light freight, such as the milk cans shown. (Courtesy of Evelyn Wicoff.)

After World War I, increased car usage caused a decline in trolley service. In December 1930, gas-electric cars replaced the electric trolleys. By November 1934, only one trip was made per day. This was done so that the electric company could keep the right-of-way and build the high-tension power lines still standing today. Trolley service stopped in May 1937. Shown here is Car No. 25, built in 1903. Notice the cowcatcher. (Courtesy of Robert Yuell.)

30

Elizabeth and Trenton Railroad Company Car No. 28 is seen on Liberty Street in Trenton c. 1912 after it came off the private right-of-way. This car serviced Plainsboro from May 18, 1910, to June 30, 1913. It was one of the six original trolley cars that would have stopped at the three Plainsboro stations. Netting on the front of the car was designed to safely catch people or animals that were accidentally struck. (Courtesy of Robert Yuell.)

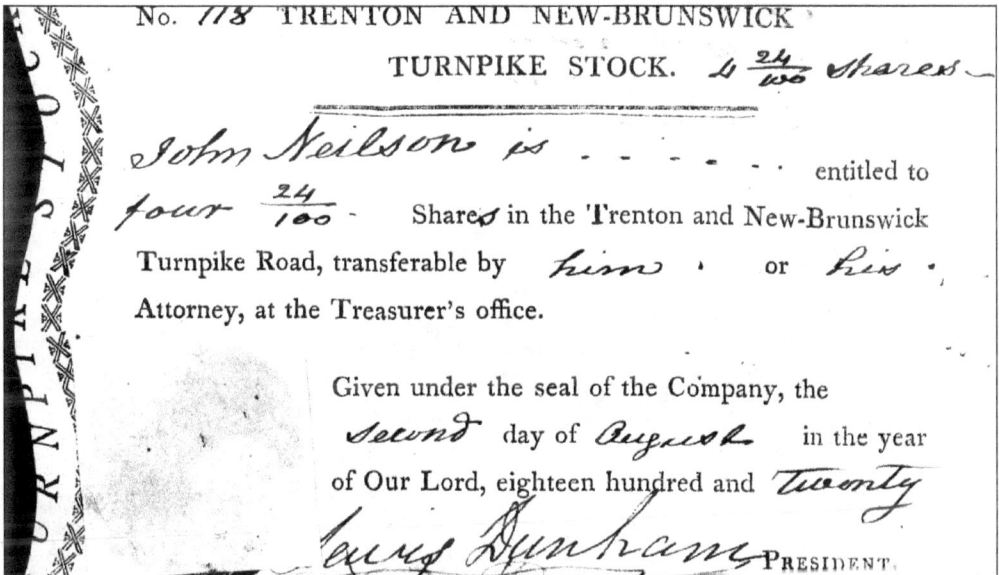

Shown is a stock certificate of the Trenton and New Brunswick Turnpike, which was a private road chartered in 1804 with a 99-year lease. It charged per cart, horse, person, sheep, and so on. Completed in 1807, it was 25 miles long and "36 feet wide, 15 feet of which were covered with about six inches of gravel. A few wooden bridges with stone abutments and piers have been erected across intervening streams." So stated Albert Gallatin, then secretary of the U.S. Treasury. (Courtesy of Robert Yuell.)

Over time, the Trenton and New Brunswick Turnpike came to be called the Straight Turnpike. In 1903, the charter was repealed and the state of New Jersey took over the road. The route was widened and graded in 1904, but most traffic continued to use Route 27. This view looks south from Mapleton Road. The Williamson wheelwright and blacksmith shops are on the right, and Plainsboro Road is on the left. (Courtesy of Robert Yuell.)

In 1915, the road was paved with macadam. In 1927, the macadam was replaced by concrete and the road was renamed Route 26. Shoulders were added, and the blacksmith and wheelwright shops shown previously were torn down. In 1932, a center passing lane was added. It was nicknamed "the death lane." The road was widened to four lanes in 1937. That same year, a grass median was added. This c. late-1950s view shows Route 1 and FMC. (Courtesy of FMC.)

In 1953, the road was officially named Route 1. Three years later, it was blacktopped. The grass median was replaced by a concrete barrier, and a jughandle and traffic light were added to the Plainsboro Road intersection. In the 1990s, the highway was widened to six lanes. This *c.* 1960s aerial view looks east and shows FMC. The farm with the silos in the upper right is the Ruedemann Farm, located on Plainsboro Road. (Courtesy of FMC.)

The Millstone River forms the southern and western boundary of Plainsboro. The river provided the power for the mills of the Aqueduct community. In 1834, when the Delaware and Raritan Canal was completed, an aqueduct was created to carry the canal over the river. It was from this aqueduct that the area derived its name. This wooden bridge was constructed to carry the Straight Turnpike over the Millstone River. This photograph was taken prior to 1906 and looks upstream. (Courtesy of Esther Engelke.)

The Delaware and Raritan Canal was constructed between 1830 and 1834. Dug almost entirely by hand by Irish immigrants, it brought new life to the members of Aqueduct community, providing them with a source of supplies and a means to ship their goods. The canal, which runs along the western border of Plainsboro, ceased operations in 1933. This *c.* 1903–1905 postcard photograph shows the workman's camp beside the canal that was used while Princeton University's Carnegie Lake was being dug. (Courtesy of Robert Yuell.)

Opened in 1951 as a 2,500-foot grass airstrip, Plainsboro's "Princeton Forrestal Campus Airfield" was modified in 1959 and again in 1977. The 3,000-foot paved runway was used by the Mechanical and Aerospace Department to test the interaction between humans and airplanes. When the project concluded, the airstrip was used by amateur fliers. Princeton University sold the land to Bristol-Myers Squibb in 1988. The runway was closed in 1991. The road running across the center of the page is Route 1.

34

Four

AROUND TOWN

For most of its life, Plainsboro was very small, with fewer than 1,000 people in 11.8 square miles. The people enjoyed the simple entertainments offered by the church and community, but to see a movie or visit a supermarket required a trip to Princeton or some other town. J.D. Van Doren's General Store was located on the south side of Plainsboro Road, just west of Edgemere Avenue. Built in the 1880s, the building was moved in the late 1930s to the Anderson Farm on Petty Road, where it was used to store potatoes. The man is unidentified but may be J.D. Van Doren. Van Doren's sold everything from canned goods to clothing. Perhaps he sold insurance too, as the sign next to the lamp reads, "The Hartford Insurance Company." The white stepping stone in the lower center of the picture, used for mounting a horse, is engraved with the name Van Doren. It is now located at the rear entrance to the Plainsboro Museum. (Courtesy of Robert Yuell.)

The Quaker Stores, better known as the Lapidus Market, was built in 1928 by J.D. Van Doren for $6,000. Subsequent owners included Charles and Mildred Place, who owned the store for 10 years. Located on the north side of Plainsboro Road, just west of Dey Road, the store was purchased from Erin Gross by Sol and Ray Lapidus of Brooklyn on December 27, 1941. The Lapidus Market stayed in business until the 1990s, gradually adding sandwiches and catering to its grocery line. (Courtesy of Stanley and Elsa Lapidus.)

The Lapidus Market was a high-quality butcher shop that sold a variety of goods. These included canned goods, fresh fruits and vegetables, and even work pants. The store also sold Esso gasoline. Pictured c. 1943 inside the store are Ray Lapidus; his wife, Sol Lapidus; and his mother, Dora Lapidus. The little boy is Harvey Lapidus, Ray and Sol's older son. After Ray and Sol retired, the store was run by Ray's son Stan and his wife, Elsa. (Courtesy of Stan Lapidus.)

The first "Plainsborough" post office was created on June 19, 1848. It was located in a building near the northwest corner of Plainsboro and Dey Roads. An 1861 map shows the post office in the third building west of Dey Road, on the north side of Plainsboro Road. Around 1900, the post office moved to the building on the left, on the south side of Plainsboro Road east of Edgemere Avenue. This postcard photograph was taken c. 1905.

The post office remained in this building from c. 1900 to September 6, 1963. At one time, the building also housed a general store. Mail delivery in Plainsboro began on July 23, 1973. Up until then, Plainsboro residents picked up their mail at the post office. The small mailbox on the far right says, "Santa's Mail Box." The house on the right belonged to Walker-Gordon and Deckers milkman Norman White. This photograph was taken in December 1962. (Courtesy of Cliff Sohl.)

The post office next moved to 410 Plainsboro Road, just east of Prospect Avenue. It remained there from September 7, 1963, to April 25, 1976. This building is now the Village Store. Pictured here is Raymond Sohl, postmaster for 17 years. The post office was relocated one last time to 12 Schalks Crossing Road, where it remains today. The photograph dates from c. 1973. (Courtesy of Ray Sohl.)

The state police barracks on Route 1 was built in the early 1950s on land donated by Princeton University. It was named for Theodore D. Parsons, former attorney general of New Jersey. Since Plainsboro did not have a police department, the state police were responsible for patrolling and responding to emergencies in town. The water tower (upper center) marks College Road. The buildings in the distance (left of the tower) are on Mapleton Road. (Courtesy of the New Jersey State Police.)

Although Plainsboro did not have a police department, the town did have a part-time constable. The constable patrolled the town, directed traffic, and crossed the schoolchildren. Shown here is Kenneth E. Robbins, who became a constable in 1952 and served over 20 years. He used his own car to patrol Plainsboro. He died of a heart attack while on duty. Robbins was proceeded by Cal Heath, who was a part-time constable and patrolled on foot. (Courtesy of Lindsay Robbins.)

Clifford Maurer of the West Windsor Police Department was appointed the first chief of police on February 1, 1978. The Plainsboro Police Department was founded in March of that year. The initial police force consisted of four members and could not supply round-the-clock coverage until more officers were hired in 1979. Pictured here in the old library are, from left to right, Mayor Peter Cantu, an unidentified man, and Chief Clifford Maurer. (Courtesy of the Plainsboro Police Department.)

The first home of the police department was the old two-room schoolhouse, which also served as a municipal court and library. Finally, the department moved into the new town hall in 1982. Pictured c. 1978 are, from left to right, Ptl. Larry Runge (first Plainsboro full-time policeman), Ptl. Don Crosby, Chief Clifford Maurer, and Ptl. Gary Coderoni. (Courtesy of the Plainsboro Police Department.)

The Plainsboro Volunteer Fire Company No. 1 was organized on December 1, 1959, and went into operation on June 18, 1960. The first truck, shown here (front), was a 1941 American LaFrance 750-gallon-per-minute pumper. It was purchased from Pennington Township. Also purchased (from Blawenburg Township) was a used Dodge 1,000-gallon booster tank truck (seen behind the fire truck). Pictured in November 1963 are John "Junior" Wills (left) and Chief Elmer Wilson. (Courtesy of John Wills.)

The fire company was first housed in a cinder-block building behind the Plainsboro Hardware Store on Plainsboro Road. In July 1962, it moved to its current location on land donated by the Wicoff family and Walker-Gordon. This c. 1969 photograph shows Plainsboro's first new truck, a 1965 Ford Hahn fire truck with a 500-gallon tank and 1,000 feet of hose. Pictured is Chief John "Junior" Wills. (Courtesy of John Wills.)

This three-bay building was constructed in 1962 with donations from the people of Plainsboro and lots of work by the volunteer fire company members. Dedicated on September 8, 1963, it was expanded again in 1975–1976 with two more bays. The vehicles shown are, from left to right, the Dodge 1,000-gallon truck, the Ford Hahn, and a Ford Power Wagon. (Courtesy of the Plainsboro Volunteer Fire Department.)

This is the five-bay Plainsboro Fire Department building that was expanded from three bays in 1975–1976. It now houses, from left to right, a command center, two larger bays for big trucks, the original three bays, and a meeting room with kitchen facilities. It was dedicated on August 12, 1978. This five-bay building was demolished, and a seven-bay firehouse was constructed. It was dedicated on October 15, 2000. (Courtesy of the Plainsboro Fire Department.)

The Forrestal campus is in some ways like a small village. The type of research conducted there required an immediate response to any emergency. Pictured in 1965 is a fire engine used by the Princeton Plasma Physics Laboratory. The truck was also equipped with hot suits and first-aid equipment. The truck is a Dodge Power Wagon with four-wheel drive. (Courtesy of the Princeton Plasma Physics Laboratory.)

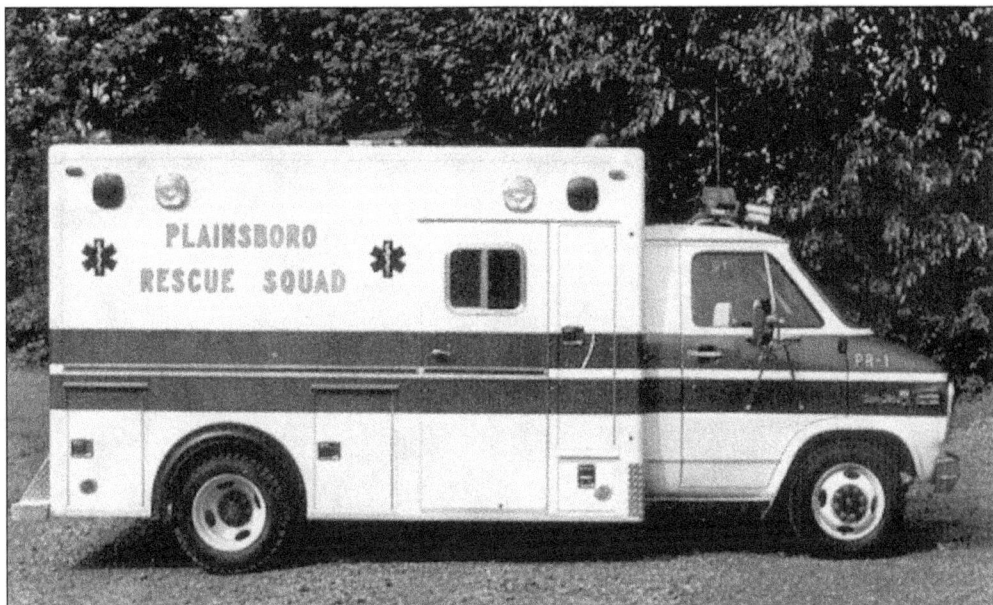

The Plainsboro Rescue Squad was founded in 1974. Art Santawasso was the first captain, and Rick Butler was the first president. The squad's first ambulance was a 1957 red Cadillac borrowed from the Cranbury First Aid Squad. The second, a white Pontiac ambulance, was purchased for $1 from the Port Reading First Aid Squad. The rescue squad truck shown here was purchased in 1978. (Courtesy of the Plainsboro Rescue Squad.)

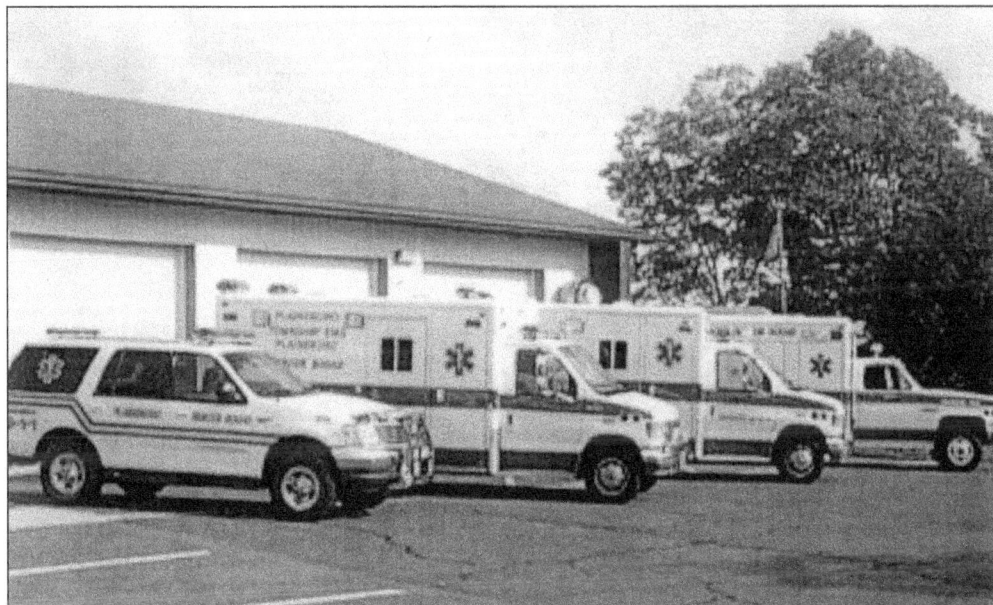

The Plainsboro Rescue Squad's first home was a garage behind the Plainsboro Hardware Store. The garage had room for the ambulances, but meetings and training had to be conducted elsewhere. In 1975, the first new ambulance was purchased. A second new ambulance was purchased in 1978, and the squad had to move to an unused equipment shed on the Walker-Gordon Farm. Shown here is the squad's current home, dedicated in June 1985. (Courtesy of the Plainsboro Rescue Squad.)

The Plainsboro Rescue Squad is a volunteer organization with three full-time emergency medical technicians (EMTs) and several per-diem EMTs. Shown here are the 1988 officers. From left to right are the following: (front row) Ann Strode, Bruce Nelson, Harriet White, Deanna Krausman, and Louise Harner; (back row) M. Rowe, G. DeForge, M. Horne, and Christopher Rowe. (Courtesy of the Plainsboro Rescue Squad.)

In addition to its own fire truck, the Princeton Plasma Physics Laboratory maintained its own rescue-squad vehicle. This heavy rescue-squad truck was an all-terrain Power Wagon equipped with a winch in front. The men in this 1968 photograph are not identified. (Courtesy of the Princeton Plasma Physics Laboratory.)

44

Originally a two-room schoolhouse, this building later housed the Plainsboro Township Hall, the municipal court, the police department, and the library. The library was founded in 1964 as an association library (with 500 books and four shelves) by Betty Jeffers, Janet Jeffers, Clarise Knight, and Priscilla Stitt. It became a municipal library in 1986 and moved to its current location in 1993. This photograph dates from c. 1973. (Courtesy of the Plainsboro Police Department.)

The municipal center was moved to the Wicoff house in 1977, when the town purchased the house and land. In 1982–1983, the township constructed an additional facility to house the court, police, and meeting rooms. In keeping with the township's roots, the building had a "barn design," including a cupola on the roof with the old Walker-Gordon cow-shaped weathervane. The hall, pictured c. 1984, was expanded in 1993, when a new municipal center and library were built. Only a part of this building was maintained in the process.

Plainsboro has long used a town committee form of government, headed by a mayor. There have been three long-term mayors of Plainsboro: John Van Buren Wicoff, Henry Jeffers Jr., and Peter Cantu. Pictured here are members of the 1981 township committee. From left to right are Rudy Wellnitz (who served one term as mayor), Constance Camner, Mayor Peter Cantu, Jack Seiber, Barbara Wright (who served two terms as mayor), and Chester Steen (township clerk and longtime employee at Walker-Gordon).

Shown c. 1932 is the office of the "Recorder and Justice of the Peace" (as seen on the sign), located in a house on the northwest corner of Plainsboro Road and Pasture Lane. The justice of the peace at that time was John Holohan. Pictured here is Jimmy Robbins. The child is believed to be Priscilla Knight Stitt. (Courtesy of Priscilla Stitt.)

Judge Holohan is pictured c. the late 1950s inside the office shown in the previous photograph. Born in 1880 in Ireland, he came to the United States c. 1905 and moved to Plainsboro in 1924. He served as a judge in Plainsboro from 1934 to 1954. Holohan also owned a trucking business until c. 1935. His trucks delivered milk for the Walker-Gordon Farm. The judge later sold the trucking firm to Russell Hullfish. (Courtesy of the Holohan family.)

In 1899, phone service came to Plainsboro when John Van Buren Wicoff, Henry Jeffers Sr., and E.L. Mount made an agreement with the Farmers and Traders Telephone Company. The agreement specified that the men mentioned above would put up the lines and switchboard and that the company would supply the service. The company was sold to Bell Telephone for $195,000 in 1930. This building, located at the southwest corner of Maple Avenue and Plainsboro Road, housed the phone exchange. (Photograph by Robert Yuell, 1991.)

The Bethel Cemetery, located on the north side of Plainsboro Road just west of the railroad bridge, may be as old as the church, which was built in 1812. However, the oldest known grave marker is that of Helene McGhee, dated May 21, 1845. The church closed in 1909. From 1954 to 1989, the Lions Club of Plainsboro maintained the cemetery. Since then, its upkeep has been conducted by the Plainsboro Historical Society. This view dates from 1955. (Photograph by Betty Wellnitz.)

This is the George Davison home, located on Plainsboro Road at the intersection of George Davison Road. The 1939 map of Plainsboro shows the George "Davidson" farm at this location encompassing 145 acres. Built in the early 1800s, the house burned down on July 12, 1981. Although four fire companies and 50 men fought the blaze, the house was destroyed. The cause was arson. The man in the photograph is identified only as "Uncle Jerry." (Courtesy of Mr. and Mrs. Nathan W. Dey.)

Pictured in 1955 is the McNamee House, located on the south side of Plainsboro Road west of the railroad bridge. This land once operated as a farm, and at one time there was a barn and a small house behind the house for use by the "hired hand." East of the house, the 1939 map shows a "McNamee Road," which led to the barns and the McNamee hay press. However, that road no longer exists. (Photograph by Betty Wellnitz.)

The Ruedemann House, shown here, was located on Plainsboro Road next to the Jeffers residence and across from the Walker-Gordon Farm. The horse barn to the right of this house was used to conduct testing for the building of the first Walker-Gordon Rotolactor. The barn burned in 1938. Prior to 1918, this was the Walker-Gordon boardinghouse for single men. The house burned and was torn down in 1991. (Courtesy of the Ruedemann family.)

The Ruedemann and Jeffers families were joined when Dana "Rudy" Ruedemann married Emily Jeffers. Shown c. 1945 are, from left to right, the following: (front row) Bill, Rudolph, and Calvin Ruedemann; (middle row) Henry Jeffers Sr., Anna Adams Jeffers, Elizabeth Hienzman Ruedemann, and Carl August Rudolph Ruedemann; (back row) Emily Jeffers Ruedemann, Emily Ruedemann, and Dana "Rudy" Ruedemann. (Courtesy of the Ruedemann family.)

This view of Prospect Avenue looks north from Edgemere Avenue. The photograph was taken in 1955, around the time that area was undergoing development. Notice that the road is still made of dirt. It was not paved until the early 1960s. The houses on the left belonged to Buddy Brooks, Lenny Luther, Clarence Cornell, and John Lacik. On the right, the houses were owned by Mike Pomianoski, Milton Shinn, and Dick Cherrington. (Photograph by Betty Wellnitz.)

In this 1955 view looking west on Plainsboro Road, Prospect Avenue is on the left. The sign reads, "Borden's Fountain," "Buck's Sandwich Shop," and "Luncheonette. Notions. Cigars. Try Our Hamburgers." Buck's was a sandwich shop and soda fountain. The building up the street, Tom and Ann's (indicated by the sign with an ice-cream cone), also contained a barbershop. Tom and Ann's was also a luncheonette and sold magazines, newspapers, notions, jewelry, and even men's clothing. (Photograph by Betty Wellnitz.)

The Walker-Gordon Pond was often called "the Duck Pond." Fed by Devil's Brook, it was created by Walker-Gordon in the early 1900s so that ice could be harvested. Here we see Henry and Anna Jeffers, with their grandchildren, feeding the ducks from the old concrete Plainsboro Road bridge. The bridge was later destroyed during a hurricane. From left to right are Emily, Bill, and Rudolph Ruedemann; Ann Jeffers; Henry Jeffers III; and Calvin Ruedemann. (Courtesy of the Ruedemann family.)

On the other side of the bridge, at the end of what is now Jeffers Road and Pasture Lane, the Walker-Gordon Pond served as a swimming hole. Seen c. 1940 on the diving board is George Luther Jr. Standing in the water is Jack Houtenville. Ted Wilson (left) and Bill Wilson are swimming. The girls are, from left to right, Jackie Cornell, Emily Ruedemann, Priscilla Knight Stitt (standing), an unidentified girl, Mary Freed, and Della Stout.

The Holiday Inn on Route 1 South, just north of Mapleton Road, was a landmark for many years. Opened in 1961, it operated as a hotel until March 31, 1990, and was later torn down. This view, looking east, shows the hotel and FMC across the highway. The land just north of where FMC now stands was referred to locally as "Wellnitz Hill" after the Wellnitz farm (owned by Walker-Gordon), which existed near there for many years. (Courtesy of FMC.)

Five

CHURCHES, SCHOOLS AND ORGANIZATIONS

As in many small towns, the church, school, and other organizations were the center of social life in Plainsboro. Clubs, committees, and sports existed for both the young and old. Founded in 1812, the Bethel Methodist Church was erected on land donated by Robert Davison Jr. on the north side of Plainsboro Road just west of where the railroad tracks would one day be constructed. The first minister was Rev. Joseph Totten. The church foundered in its early years and fell into disrepair, but it was restored and reopened in 1850. Attendance declined again when the circuit minister changed the Sunday service to the afternoon. Finally, in 1909, services were discontinued. The building, shown in this c. 1912 postcard, was abandoned. It was torn down by the town c. 1936.

Plainsboro's second church, shown in this c. 1914 postcard, was a nondenominational structure built on the southeast corner of Plainsboro Road and Parkway Avenue in 1879. Founded by Rev. John Miller of Princeton, the church was called the Miller Church, the Evangelical Church of Plainsboro, and the Trustees of the Congregation of the Old Church of Plainsborough (its incorporated name). The vestibule and steeple were added in 1898. The building on the left is the church manse, constructed in 1913. (Courtesy of Evelyn Wicoff.)

In 1907, the church was reorganized as the United Presbyterian Church. The original church was replaced in 1933 by a stone building, but the first church was relocated to the back of the property and used as a parish hall. The new church was dedicated on June 18, 1933. In 1984, an addition was added to the back of the church, but the original 1879 church, visible on the left, was maintained. This photograph is dated May 24, 1939.

54

The date of construction of the Mapleton School, shown here, is not known, but it does appear in the records of 1880 as having 46 children attending. It was located in the Mapleton section of Plainsboro on the west side of Route 1, a half-mile north of Plainsboro Road. It ceased to be a school in the 1920s and was moved to the east side of Route 1 to be used as a farm building. (Collection of the Historical Society of Princeton.)

Other one-room schoolhouses were known to have existed in Plainsboro. They stood on the northeast corner of Dey and Scotts Corner Roads, near the southwest corner of George Davison and Plainsboro Roads, on Cranbury Neck Road near the bend leading to Grovers Mill, and on the west side of Schalks Crossing Road north of Plainsboro Road. This c. 1914 postcard view shows the two-room schoolhouse, located on the south side of Plainsboro Road, west of Parkway Avenue. The church manse, constructed in 1913, is on the right. (Courtesy of Robert Yuell.)

The two-room schoolhouse was constructed in 1908; however, a school building also appears on an 1876 map near this location. This is perhaps the most important landmark in Plainsboro history since it was the controversy over the condition of the schools that led to Plainsboro's founding. This photograph is dated September 1910. Today the building houses the West Windsor–Plainsboro School District's Special Services.

Plainsboro's four-room schoolhouse, shown here, was dedicated on September 24, 1924. In 1960, an addition was made to the school. Another addition was added in 1975, at which time the name of the school was changed to the John Van Buren Wicoff School in order to honor the man who had been head of the Plainsboro Board of Education from 1919 to 1950. This photograph is dated May 24, 1939.

Plainsboro had no senior high school and a seventh and eighth grade only until the 1940s. Sixth-grade graduates were sent to Princeton to continue their education. In 1969, Plainsboro and West Windsor joined forces to create a junior and senior high school system, which is now one of the best in New Jersey. Since it was started over an education dispute, Plainsboro is sometimes called "the Education Township." This *c.* 1924 school photograph was taken inside the four-room school building.

The 102-acre Hillcrest Farms was purchased on July 1, 1912, from Samuel and Harriet Fishburn by the Congregation of the Mission of St. Vincent de Paul (Vincentians) to build a minor seminary called St. Joseph's College. Two buildings, Slattery Hall and St. Joseph's Seminary, were completed in 1914 and are shown here in a rear view looking toward Carnegie Lake, at the top of the photograph. Likly Gymnasium, in the foreground, was added in 1916. (Courtesy of St. Joseph's College.)

In 1918, the college bought the 73-acre William E. Foote farm so that its land now ran along College Road from the canal to the east side of Route 1. The 17 acres east of Route 1 were sold in 1960, and another 108 acres west of Route 1 were sold in 1984. This c. 1935 postcard view shows the seminary with the Queen of the Miraculous Medal Chapel and sacristy (far right), added in 1934. Likly Gymnasium, which burned, has been rebuilt. (Courtesy of Chris Reef.)

St. Joseph's College was a minor seminary, educating both high school and college boys. The school consisted of four years of high school and four years of college. By 1940, the college junior and senior years were discontinued. In 1970, the freshman and sophomore college classes ended. The high school closed in 1992. Today, the college operates primarily as a retreat and renewal center. This photograph is from the 1955 yearbook. (Courtesy of St. Joseph's College.)

In August 1925, seven members of the Missionary Sisters of the Precious Blood arrived at the seminary to take over domestic duties. They occupied the old Fishburn farmhouse, pictured here, and renamed it the Convent of St. Theresa of the Child Jesus. Two buildings—St. Vincent's Hall and Skelly Hall—were added to the seminary in 1961. The sisters then moved into Slattery Hall, and the convent was torn down. The sisters left St. Joseph's in 1981. (Courtesy of Chris Reef.)

Constructed in 1883 as a one-floor structure and used as a school and town meeting place, the Grange Hall was jacked up in 1914 and converted to two stories. The school continued on the "second" floor until the new four-room schoolhouse was constructed. The Plainsboro Grange, organized on December 19, 1908, met here. Located on the south side of Plainsboro Road and west of J.D. Van Doren's General Store, the building burned to the ground on February 17, 1928. (Courtesy of Robert Yuell.)

Pictured here is the prayer at the groundbreaking ceremony of the Mechanics Hall, built at 501 Plainsboro Road. Looking south from an unpaved Schalks Crossing Road, this c. 1928–1929 view shows, from left to right, a corner of Dr. Guy Dean Jr.'s house, the two-room schoolhouse, the brick Presbyterian church manse, and the wood-frame Presbyterian church. Built at a cost of about $5,000, this was the home of Plainsboro Council No. 299 of the Junior Order of United American Mechanics. (Courtesy of Marjorie Jacobsen.)

Founded on April 9, 1912, Plainsboro Council No. 299 of the Junior Order of United American Mechanics met in the Grange Hall before this building was completed in 1929. The building was dedicated on September 29, 1929. An auditorium was added that same year. Besides meetings, the hall was used for dinners, dances, movies, bingo games, and plays. Located on the corner of Plainsboro and Schalks Crossing Roads, the building was sold on June 10, 1957. Plainsboro Council No. 299 was merged on September 27, 1982, with another council. (Courtesy of Marjorie Jacobsen.)

This photograph shows the cast of *Old Fashioned Choir*, a play performed in the Mechanics Hall on June 16, 1935. From left to right are the following: (front row) Julia Chamberlin, Jessica Eckles, Mrs. Glenn Ousley, unidentified, Mabel McKenzie, and ? Redfield; (back row) J. Russell Britton, Elsie Atwood, Logan Wilson, Minnie Sohl, unidentified, Marge Jacobsen, Meta Hudler, unidentified, Cora Sayler, Mary Franklin, Nellie White, Clarice Knight, unidentified, Paul Hudley, and "Pop" Carwile. (Courtesy of Marjorie Jacobsen.)

The Ladies Aid organization is shown on the steps of the Presbyterian church manse *c.* 1920. From left to right are the following: (front row) Mary Coy Bolles, ? Taft, Louise Britton, Nellie White (holding Norman), Mrs. George Davison, and Irene Barlow Grover; (middle row) ? Eckles, Lavinia Applegate Wicoff, May Petty, Margaret Britton, Mamie Davison, Etta Britton Johnson, Mrs. Harvey Grover, Lillie Barlow Perrine, and Olive Horton Bolles (holding Daniel); (back row) Gertrude Benard, Margaret Hullfish Daly, May ?, Mrs. Jake Hultz, and ? Bullock. (Courtesy of Rudy A. Wellnitz.)

This photograph of the Plainsboro First Aid Group was taken in the Rotolactor record room at the Walker-Gordon Farm in 1942. The group may have been formed in response to World War II. They are as follows: (front row) Clara Cornell (2nd from left), Berdina Bolles (4th), and ? Applegate (8th); (middle row) Leon Wilson (1st), Clarice Knight (3rd), Elsie Morris (8th), and Harry A. Stults (10th); (back row) Logan Wilson (1st), Edna Atwood (2nd), Lee Clark (4th), Chet Mowery (6th), Marge Jacobsen (7th), and Dora Ellis (11th). Seated on the floor is William Davidson. Notice the cow record cards behind the group.

This photograph, dated September 19, 1955, shows the Peppy Pals, a local girls' club. Clockwise, starting with the woman in the chair, are Jenny Belle Clark, Linda Pendyke, Lynda Moyer Hafenmaier, Donna Pendyke, Sandra Britton, Judy Parker, Cissy Dean, "Chucky" Slider, Tina Strode, Gayle Thompson Cantu, and Carolyn Lampkin. (Courtesy of the Clark family.)

Originally Troop No. 68, Plainsboro's Boy Scout troop became No. 168 in the late 1950s. Pictured *c.* 1942 in a memorial service for Sam Grace at the Walker-Gordon Farm are, from left to right, Scoutmaster Charles Luther Jr., Jack Houtenville, Billy Murphy, unidentified, John Warner, Joseph Lacik, Grover Perrine, Frank Hale, Mike Kostue, Amos Hamlett, George Luther Jr., Walter Lacik, and William Perrine. Grace had been the leader of Troop No. 68 but was killed in North Africa in 1942.

These Plainsboro Boy Scouts from Troop No. 168 are on their way to a jamboree in Colorado Springs *c.* 1960. From left to right are Scoutmaster Charles Luther Jr. and Scouts Robert Luther, Jerry Hullfish, Barry Smith, David Hullfish, Lindsay Robbins, Bruce Tippi, Raymond Hullfish, and Bob Watlington. Barry Smith later died in the Vietnam War. (Courtesy of the David Hullfish family.)

The Lions Club of Plainsboro was chartered on April 29, 1954. This photograph, taken *c.* 1960, is from a joint meeting with the West Windsor chapter. Seated on the left is Dr. Guy Dean Jr., longtime resident physician of Plainsboro. The others are unidentified. (Courtesy of Robert Allison.)

This photograph from 1922 shows the Four M's Club (a boys' club) camping at the Jeffers Farm at Kingsley, Pennsylvania. In the front row are, from left to right, unidentified, John Major, William Groendyke Jr., and Douglas Wicoff (the rest unidentified). Third from the left in the middle row is John E. Wicoff. From left to right in the back row are John Van Buren Wicoff, Henry W. Jeffers Sr., Betsy M. Oakley Jeffers, Adelade Jeffers, Henry W. Jeffers Jr., and Raymond Eckels (First Presbyterian pastor).

Taken in September 1924, this photograph shows the MDC (Mr. Duryee's Club). They had just presented the bulletin board seen here to the Plainsboro Presbyterian Church. The man in the upper left is Rev. Raymond Eckels. The man in the upper right is William B. Duryee, the club leader. The club also put on shows in the Grange Hall and was dissolved by 1930. A boy had to be 10 years old to join. (Courtesy of Marjorie Jacobsen.)

Plainsboro had baseball teams from 1935 to 1954. The Plainsboro teams were part of the "Twin-M League," which stood for "Middlesex and Mercer." Plainsboro had four teams over the years: Walker-Gordon Laboratories (WGL), Walker-Gordon, and Plainsboro. These last two teams combined to form the fourth team called Walker-Gordon-Plainsboro. Pictured here is Milton H. "Shinny" Shinn, who played for Walker-Gordon Laboratories in the 1930s. (Collection of Phyllis DiFrancesco.)

Pictured c. 1946 is the Walker-Gordon baseball team. From left to right are the following: (front row) Buddy Brooks, Harold Britton, Ray Simonson, John Boyko, Bus Simonson, Ollie Boyko (who went on to play minor-league baseball), Mike Mayfarth, Joe Kirby, and Joe Friel; (back row) Henry Jeffers Jr. (sponsor), Joe Mozgo, Adam Boyko, Ken Robbins, Rudy Mozgo, and Bruce Ferguson (manager). (Courtesy of John Boyko.)

This photograph shows the 1955 Princeton YMCA Little League champion Plainsboro Pirates. From left to right are the following: (front row) Henry Schmidts, Douglas Cormack, Stanley Lupidus, Jerry Hullfish, and Jamie Thompson; (middle row) Jack Britton, Ronnie O'Brien, Bob Watlington, Dale Campbell, and Jim Lovelace; (back row) Chet Steen (manager), Jim Sassman, Walter Stalcup, Walter Bronson, Alvin Anderson, Guy Thompson, Bill Libby, and Dan Daley (coach). Formed in 1953, the Pirates won the championship in 1955, 1956, and 1957. (Courtesy of Jack Britton.)

Although Plainsboro had no high school, it did have a high-school basketball team. Pictured here is the St. Joseph College High School team from 1955. The Vincentians were undefeated in their 10-game season, beating larger high schools, such as Seton Hall, twice along the way. The St. Joseph boys also played intramural sports, swam in the canal in the summer, and played hockey on the canal in winter. (Courtesy of St. Joseph's College.)

Like most farm towns, Plainsboro had a 4-H organization. Pictured in 1952 are, from left to right, Judy Parker, Robert Troise (game warden), Donald MacKenzie, and Matt Hafenmaier. These three teenagers raised pheasants, about 250 each, which were then sold to New Jersey to be set free in the woods for hunters. The requirements for raising the birds were very strict. (Courtesy of Matt Hafenmaier.)

The Gospel Fellowship Church met in the Stanton Clark home, the firehouse, and the town hall before purchasing the old Russell Britton farm, at 626 Plainsboro Road, in 1985. The farmhouse was used as a manse, and the barn was turned into a church. Much of the original barn materials were preserved in the remodeling. The "church made from a barn" was dedicated in May 1994. (Courtesy of Stanton Clark.)

One of the most recent additions to Plainsboro is the Princeton Alliance Church. Founded in 1983, the Princeton Alliance Church was located on Route 1 South in South Brunswick from November 5, 1989, until coming to Plainsboro on March 28, 1999. Located on the northwest corner of Schalks Crossing and Scudders Mill Roads, the church is in the process of building a new addition for its growing congregation. (Courtesy of the Princeton Alliance Church.)

Six

FARMS

Plainsboro was founded as a farming community. Fertile land, plenty of water, and proximity to market all made the village an ideal location to raise crops. Over the years, the farms changed hands through deaths and sales. The size and shape changed too, making the process of following the lineage confusing at best. When Walker-Gordon came in 1897, the company began to buy huge tracts of land, which it then rented to farmers to grow silage exclusively for Walker-Gordon cows. This photograph shows the Groendyke Farm, which was located on the east side of Schalks Crossing Road. The farm was originally owned by Richard and Rachel Lake. Johannes Groendyke moved onto the farm when he married Sarah Lake c. 1745. Johannes's son Samuel then purchased the farm from the Lakes in 1785, when his father died. Pictured here in front of the farmhouse are, from left to right, John S.V. Groendyke, Luella M. Groendyke, Cornelia V. Groendyke, and William B. Groendyke. (Courtesy of Marjorie Groendyke Jacobsen.)

Samuel Groendyke died childless in 1816, and his nephew Richard purchased the farm. Richard, in turn, divided the 152-acre farm between his two sons. John Story Groendyke retained the original "homestead" property with the house. John passed the farm on to his son, but it was another son, William B. Groendyke, who actually farmed the land. The people pictured here in front of an enlarged farmhouse are probably William B., his wife Cornelia V., and a servant. (Courtesy of Clare and Rita Humphrey.)

The original Lake home, built c. 1740, had a central hall and servants' quarters and has since been torn down. A new home was built sometime after 1850, a bit closer to the road. The farm grew potatoes, rye, wheat, hay, and corn. In 1924, the Groendykes gave up farming. The land then passed to Walker-Gordon, from there to Bill Dennison, and finally to the Parker family. The 1850 home, seen in the distance on the right, has been torn down. (Courtesy of Marjorie Groendyke Jacobsen.)

The Simonson farm began in Plainsboro in 1920, when the family purchased farmland on Dey Road. Edward Simonson Sr. and Martha Bammann Simonson, who met in New York City, married in 1912. They moved to Etra in 1914 and grew potatoes on the Vandeveer farm. They then farmed in Sharon and Windsor before moving to Plainsboro. Pictured c. 1935 is Edward "Bus" Simonson Jr. on an Emerson Brantingham tractor built c. 1915. (Courtesy of Edward "Bus" Simonson Jr.)

Edward Simonson Sr. died in 1921. In 1924, the family moved to Absecon, but "uncle" Ted Bammann remained to work the farm. Edward's sons Bus and Ray helped Bammann during the summers. The Simonsons moved back to Plainsboro in 1932. Pictured c. 1920 in front of their farmhouse are, from left to right, Ted Bammann, Edward "Bus" Simonson (born in 1915), Ray Simonson (born in 1917), Louise Bammann, Frieda Bammann, and Marjorie Simonson Girth. The woman on the porch is unidentified. (Courtesy of Edward "Bus" Simonson Jr.)

The Simonson brothers grew corn and rye. In 1935, they began to grow potatoes. By 1940, some 300 acres were devoted to that crop. Five acres were devoted to Christmas trees in 1952. The Simonsons then began to add acreage. The Christmas trees eventually covered 125 acres. Today, people travel many miles each year to visit the Simonson farm and cut their own Christmas tree. This is a photograph of the farmhouse from the 1930s. (Courtesy of Edward "Bus" Simonson Jr.)

The Stults farm came to Plainsboro in 1915, when Clifford Addison Stults purchased 93 acres near Cranbury Neck Road and what later became George Davison Road. They grew wheat and potatoes. Shown in this *c.* 1920s photograph is a hired hand loading 75-pound bags of potatoes onto a wagon on the Stults Farm. (Courtesy of the Stults family.)

Clifford Addison Stults's son Stanley C. Stults began farming with his father in 1944. In 1966, he acquired the farm from his father's estate. Stanley's son Stanley C. Stults Jr. joined his father two years later. They added soybeans to the wheat and potatoes. In 1971, Stanley C. Stults Jr. married Jill Ellen Roszel. The Stultses began to lease farmland, renting 600 acres. Pictured in this *c.* 1920s view is a Stults potato harvest. The two-horse wagon shown earlier can be seen in the background. (Courtesy of the Stults family.)

In 1984, Stanley C. Stults Sr. retired. Leasing farmland was becoming more difficult as developers purchased more land. That same year, the Stultses added "pick-your-own" crops to their production. In 1990, the Stults farm became the first Middlesex County farm permanently preserved through the Farmland Preservation Program. As of 1998, the 200-acre farm, worked solely by the Stults family, is a popular pick-your-own farm. The farmhouse, on Cranbury Neck and George Davison Roads, is seen in the background. This photograph was taken *c.* the 1960s. (Courtesy of the Stults family.)

In January 1936, George and Doris Parker purchased the 30-acre Chandler Farm on Schalks Crossing Road. The Chandlers had been unsuccessful in the poultry business and were forced to sell. When the Chandlers owned the farm, it was called the "Bungalow Poultry Farm," nicknamed as such for the original "bungalow" farmhouse shown in this c. 1937 photograph. The Parkers later purchased 93 acres from Walker-Gordon. The farm housed 20,000 chickens. (Courtesy of Doris Parker.)

The Parkers had never farmed, although George had attended an agricultural program at Rutgers and interned one year on the Forsgate Farm. However, they were successful poultry farmers, selling white eggs from their white Leghorn chickens. The Parkers added another 122 acres and ran their farm from 1936 to 1959. Shown here is George Parker on his first John Deere B 1936 tractor. The photograph is dated March 28, 1939. (Courtesy of Doris Parker.)

The Parkers worked closely with the Rutgers Agriculture Extension. They tried innovative techniques and developed one of the first mechanized egg-retrieval systems. They helped to invent a new method for washing eggs. They even once tried putting tiny red glasses on their chickens to cut down on cannibalization in the flock. (The theory was to stop the chickens from seeing blood.) Phyllis Parker (left) and Judy Parker are shown in the incubator room c. 1946. (Courtesy of Doris Parker.)

This 1940s photograph shows Doris Parker in front of the chicken coop that housed the egg-retrieval system. During World War II, the Parkers received a government contract to produce fertile eggs. These eggs were used to develop vaccines for the troops. Besides chickens, the Parkers raised some corn and wheat. In 1959, competition from the south forced the Parkers out of business. They sold their farm in 1976. Today, it is the Princeton Collection. Parker Road is named for the family. (Courtesy of Doris Parker.)

The Brittons came to America sometime before 1660 and to Plainsboro c. 1750. Col. Dean Britton (1795–1870) died without a will, and his holdings were sold by his six children. Catherine Lucretia Britton purchased the land that later became the Wicoff farm on Plainsboro Road. Across the street, her brother John Dean Britton purchased a second farm. Shown c. 1922 are, from left to right, Catherine Lucretia Britton Wicoff, Nathaniel Britton, and his wife, Becky. Nathaniel was mayor of Plainsboro from 1920 to 1922. (Courtesy of the Wicoff family.)

Shown in this c. 1930s view is the Col. Dean Britton home, also known as the Rue Farm and later owned by Bernard Brandon. The entrance to the house was off Dey Road, but it faced Plainsboro Road. After his father's death, Nathaniel stayed at this location. The land was eventually sold to developers, and the house was torn down to make room for the Princeton Meadows Golf Course. (Courtesy of Charles Rue.)

John Russell Britton inherited the farm on Plainsboro Road from his father, John Dean Britton. He, in turn, left it to his son Harold Britton c. 1959. The Brittons raised potatoes, wheat, and corn. Harold sold the farm in 1969 to Lincoln Properties. Today the farm is the Fox Run development. The house and barn were sold to the Gospel Fellowship Church. The house, which faces Plainsboro Road, was built in 1900 for $1,500. This view dates from c. 1960. (Courtesy of Jack and Sue Britton.)

The Wicoff farm was located on Plainsboro Road, east of Schalks Crossing Road, and stretched across Dey Road and what is today Scudders Mill Road. The land was farmed on shares by a resident farmer. The primary crop was potatoes. This photograph, taken c. 1920, shows potatoes being harvested on the Wicoff farm. The sack on the lower right says, "150 Lbs. Net When Packed." (Courtesy of the Wicoff family.)

The Major farm was located on the west side of Schalks Crossing Road near the intersection of Devil's Brook and the Pennsylvania Railroad tracks. It dates from the last quarter of the 18th century. The people in this c. 1890s photograph are unidentified, but the fourth man from the left may be John Major. (Courtesy of Marjorie Groendyke Jacobsen.)

The Titus family owned a home to the northeast of the Major Farm on Schalks Crossing Road. The 1876 map shows R. Titus. The Tituses were descendants of a slave named Titus, who ran away from Shrewbury in November 1775 and settled near Kendall Park. The Titus family grew vegetables, raised chickens, and operated the railroad gate at Schalks Crossing. Pictured here are Sarah Jane Titus (left) and Eloise Titus, who worked on the Groendyck Farm. (Courtesy of Marjorie Groendyke Jacobsen.)

The Okeson Farm, known as "the Crow's Nest," was located on Plainsboro Road just north of the Devil's Brook and Bethel Church. The name W. Okeson appears at this location on the 1876 map. The Okeson Farm was eventually sold to Walker-Gordon. Shown c. the 1890s in front of the farmhouse are, from left to right, unidentified; Bethenia Okeson; Bethenia's husband, William; William Okeson Jr.; Sumner Okeson; and unidentified. The black woman near the door is unidentified. (Courtesy of Charles Jones.)

This Okeson family photograph was taken in front of the same farmhouse in 1895 for the christening of Willard "Buck" Okeson. From left to right are Bethenia McCutchan Okeson, three unidentified, Rooney Dey (wearing hat), Emily Dey, Willard "Buck" Okeson (baby), unidentified, Sally Leggitt Dey (holding baby), unidentified, Mandy Okeson, unidentified (little girl), Nellie Hollenbeck White (behind girl), Lizzie Dey Okeson (against post), unidentified, Sumner Okeson, Charlie Okeson, Willie Leggitt, William Okeson Jr., and William Okeson Sr. (Courtesy of Charles Jones.)

The Nostrand family moved to this Plainsboro farm in 1913 on a Pennsylvania Railroad freight car. There were no tractors, so all operations were performed by the three teams of horses. The main cash crops were potatoes and grain. Hay and corn were grown for the horses. The Nostrands also raised cows, pigs, and chickens. The family was nearly self-sufficient. The farm was later purchased by the Pollak family. This photograph was taken c. the 1960s. (Courtesy of Paul Pollak.)

Hay is being lifted into the Nostrand barn c. the 1930s. The horses would raise the hay on a pulley, and it would then be swung into the barn and hooked on a "trolley." The hay would be moved along the trolley into the barn, where it would be dropped. The people in the photograph are unidentified. The horses are standing in front of the framing for a windmill. (Courtesy of Jean Nostrand.)

80

This c. 1916 photograph shows the Brunner Farm, located on the north side of Cranbury Neck Road, just west of George Davison Road near the intersection of Nostrand Road. Originally built c. 1840 by the Grover family, the farm was sold to the Brunners in 1916. The Brunners made extensive renovations to the house and grew potatoes and apples on the 128-acre farm. In 1969, the farm was sold to the Poling family. (Courtesy of the Brunner and Poling families.)

The Ruedemann Farm was located on both sides of Plainsboro Road, west of Walker-Gordon Pond. A small culvert leading underneath Plainsboro Road allowed the cows to travel back and forth between the farm sections. The Ruedemanns were enterprising dairy farmers. Dana "Rudy" Ruedemann created a loose housing barn for the cows. Later, he jacked up his silos and converted them into "self-feeder silos." In this photograph, Plainsboro Road runs from the upper left to the lower right. (Courtesy of FMC.)

The William Sayler Farm was located on the north side of Grovers Mill Road, just east of Maple Avenue. Sixty-nine acres in size, the farm grew potatoes. Cora Sayler, William's wife, worked at Walker-Gordon, hosing down cows, and stumped the panelists on *What's My Line?* with that occupation. Cora Lane is named for her. Today, the Sayler Farm houses the West Windsor–Plainsboro Middle School. (The house is seen on the left c. 1955.) (Photograph by Betty Wellnitz.)

The Alvin L. Anderson Farm was located on the southwest corner of Dey and Scotts Corner Roads. (The Andersons also owned 78 acres at Dey and Petty Roads.) Alvin Anderson Sr. and, later, his son Alvin Anderson Jr. raised potatoes and wheat on the 52-acre farm. The farm was later sold to Lincoln Properties and today houses the Pheasant Hollow Apartments. The house, shown here c. the 1960s, was torn down in the late 1970s. (Collection of Burtis Anderson.)

Located on the east side of Scotts Corner Road, north of Dey Road, was the 76-acre Petty Farm. It was purchased by William H. Petty Sr. in 1892 and was sold to his son William Petty Jr. in 1905. William Petty Jr.'s son Russell S. Petty took over the farm in 1966. Joseph Petty owned a 55-acre farm on the south side of Dey Road east of Petty Road. Petty Road is named for the family. The William H. Petty farmhouse is shown in this photograph. (Courtesy of Dorothy Petty Dey.)

William Petty Jr. grew potatoes, corn, soybeans, rye, and wheat. The Pettys tried planting sweet potatoes and peanuts but were unsuccessful. William Petty Jr. also managed the road maintenance for Plainsboro Township. Shown working on the William Petty Jr. Farm in 1934 is Russell S. Petty. Russell's son-in-law Gordon A. Dey farmed the land until most of it was sold to Sharbell Developers in the late 1990s. (Courtesy of Dorothy Petty Dey.)

The 94-acre Pieri Farm was located on the northwest corner of Scotts Corner and Dey Roads. The house was built prior to 1800, as evidenced by a sale on November 17, 1800. The Deys sold the farm to the Perrines, who in turn sold it to Cristina Pieri in 1927. The house, originally a wood-frame structure, had brick veneer added after the 1927 sale. Records show that when the Deys owned the land, they grew corn, oats, rye, wheat, potatoes, sweet potatoes, and apples. (Courtesy of Tina Peck.)

This farm, located on what is now the Plainsboro Preserve, was owned by Chamberlain and Barclay. It was farmed by a tenant farmer named Ludwig Magnani, who is shown here in the summer of 1929 digging potatoes with a horse team (not seen). (Courtesy of Rose Magnani Eller.)

The Joseph Magnani family worked the E.S. Barclay Farm. This 126-acre farm was located on the west side of Scotts Corner Road, along Shallow Brook. Shown in this 1929 photograph is Joseph Magnani digging potatoes with a four-horse-hitch one-row potato digger. (Courtesy of Rose Magnani Eller.)

Shown here is the Joseph Magnani house at the E.S. Barclay Farm. Tenant farmers were not uncommon in Plainsboro. Many tenant farmers worked for Walker-Gordon. This photograph was taken in 1951. Notice the chicken in the yard and the kitten at the foot of the door on the left. (Courtesy of Rose Magnani Eller.)

The Wilson Farm was located south of the Sayler property off Grovers Mill Road. Today, the West Windsor–Plainsboro North High School is located there. The farm gained national fame in 1938 from Orson Welles's *War of the Worlds* radio broadcast. In that play, Welles had Martians landing on the Wilmuth Farm, a nonexistent property. The next day, reporters swarmed to the Wilson Farm, assuming its name had been mispronounced in the broadcast. (Courtesy of Plainsboro Township.)

There were many small farms and farmhouses along Route 1, most of which were owned by the Rockefeller Institute for Medical Research. Route 1 is shown in a view looking north. On the left side of the highway, from bottom to top, are the Hawke Farm, the Ring Farm, the Dr. Sayre house (today this is Sayre Drive), and the Smillie Farm. On the right is the Jamieson Farm. (Courtesy of FMC.)

Princeton Nurseries were located on Mapleton Road, north of College Road, and extended into South Brunswick (Kingston). It was started c. 1912 by William Flemer Sr., who bought four contiguous farms from the Gullick, Higgins, Myrick, and Pullen families, totaling 265 acres. The business grew to be the largest wholesale nursery in the world. Its stock was sold all over the world and helped reforest Europe after World War II. This photograph dates from c. 1926. (Courtesy of Bill Flemer III.)

This 1985 aerial view shows Princeton Nurseries on the left along Mapleton Road. Carnegie Lake and the Delaware and Raritan Canal cross the bottom of the photograph. St. Joseph's Seminary is the large structure in the lower center, and to its left is College Road. On the right, Princeton Landing is being constructed. In the upper right is Princeton headquarters of the New Jersey State Troopers. Route 1 runs from the upper left to the upper right. (Courtesy of the Princeton Forrestal Center.)

This photograph shows the stucco farmhouse just south of St. Joseph's Seminary on Mapleton Road. Like Route 1, there were once many such farmhouses along Mapleton Road. Pictured c. 1935 are, from left to right, John Reef, unidentified, Marty Reef, Joe Reef (young boy), Mary Reef, and Hermann Reef. (Courtesy of Chris Reef.)

The Wellnitz family moved to Plainsboro in 1932 to operate a 300-acre farm owned by Walker-Gordon. Walker-Gordon rented land to farmers who, in turn, had a contract to sell the feed crops back to Walker-Gordon. The Wellnitz farm was on the east side of Route 1, north of Plainsboro Road (where FMC is today). The little knoll came to be called "Wellnitz Hill." Pictured c. the late 1930s are Rudy A. Wellnitz and his wife, Olive Bolles Wellnitz. (Courtesy of Rudy B. Wellnitz.)

Rudy A. Wellnitz was one of eight "crop unit men" who grew alfalfa and corn for Walker-Gordon. He also grew wheat and vegetables as cash crops. In 1955, when the land was sold to FMC, the Wellnitz family moved to another farm. Son Rudy B. Wellnitz joined his father as a partner in 1947, eventually farming 800 acres for Walker-Gordon. Shown c. 1940 are, from left to right, children Julia, Rudy B., Bruce, and Eugene Wellnitz. (Courtesy of Rudy B. Wellnitz.)

Plainsboro was innovative in improving farm equipment. The Brandon Brothers were also "crop unit men" for Walker-Gordon. They are shown c. the 1950s operating an eight-row corn planter that they created by rigging two four-row International planters together. Bernie and Curt grew corn silage for Walker-Gordon for many years. The brothers also rigged three fertilizer spreaders together to use on this 1,200-acre farm.

The men in this late-1942 photograph are crop farming for Walker-Gordon. Here they are using a John Deere A tractor to pull a Fox Forage Harvester. They are harvesting alfalfa. The harvester would cut the alfalfa into one-and-one-half-inch pieces and then pull it up and dump it into the truck. The man driving the tractor may be Daniel Bolles.

Walker-Gordon decentralized its farming operations in 1924 and created "crop unit men." There were eight such men, and each farmed approximately 300 acres. These unidentified men are crop farming for Walker-Gordon c. the 1930s. They are using a hay loader pulled by a truck. A series of teeth grabbed the hay, and arms pulled it up onto the loader bed. The men then pulled the hay off the loader and onto the truck.

This man, who may be Rudy A. Wellnitz, is driving a John Deere two-cylinder tractor made in the 1920s. It is distinctive in its iron wheels. The tractor is pulling a mower and hay rake. The mower cuts the hay, and the rake pulls the hay into rows so that it can be picked up by the hay loader.

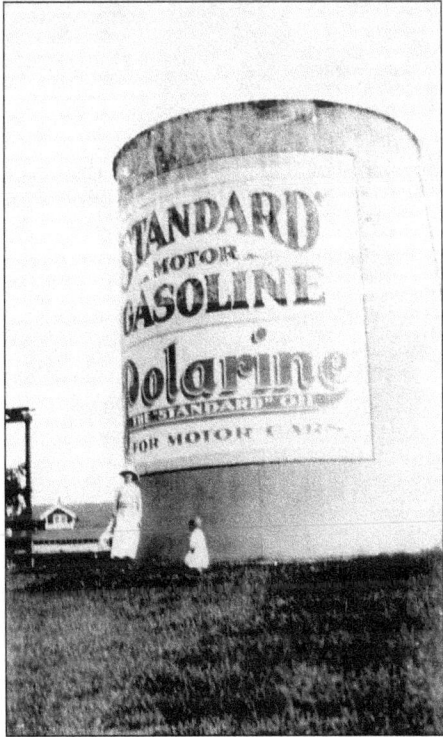

To keep all that farm equipment moving required fuel. Most farms maintained their own fuel tanks, sometimes one for gasoline and a second for diesel. Plainsboro was also a fuel-distribution center. Standard Oil kept large tanks along the Pennsylvania Railroad tracks in Plainsboro. These tanks were located on the west side of the tracks just south of the Plainsboro High Bridge. This photograph was taken c. the 1920s. (Courtesy of Ray Sohl.)

Plainsboro farmers did not have far to go to purchase equipment. In 1914, Isaac Barlow Jr. (1876–1941), who worked as a farmer for Walker-Gordon, opened up a farm-equipment business on Plainsboro Road across from the post office. Isaac sold John Deere tractors and implements. In 1934, Isaac's son Edward J. Barlow joined his father in the business. Five years later, Isaac retired and the business was taken over by Edward. Over the years, additional items were added to the product line. They included coal, feed, Allis Chalmers tractors, Massey-Harris tractors, Willys Jeeps, and Texaco gasoline. Edward also owned a small fleet of airplanes at Trenton Airport in the early 1940s, but the airport closed in 1942 because of the war. Edward died in 1953, and the business was continued by his son Robert Barlow Sr.; Edward's wife, Catherine; and Edward's daughters Catherine (Sis), Elizabeth (Betty), and Diane (Cookie). This 1952 photograph shows Edward J. Barlow in front of his John Deere dealership. The car is Edward's new 1952 Lincoln Capri. Today, Plainsboro Hardware and Casa Rosario's Restaurant occupy this building. (Courtesy of Robert Barlow Sr.)

Seven

RESEARCH

The name Plainsboro evokes thoughts of vast farms and herds of dairy cows, but not research. Surprisingly, however, extensive research took place in this town, and it continues today. Some of it was agricultural, but nuclear, chemical, aerodynamic, weather, and biological research all occurred in Plainsboro. Plainsboro became a research town in 1916, when the New York Rockefeller Institute for Medical Research organized its department of animal pathology for the study of animal diseases and moved it to Plainsboro. The institute purchased about 800 acres of land on both sides of Route 1, north of Plainsboro Road. About 500 of the acres were used to grow food for the animals. This c. 1920s photograph shows the power plant (center left, with the large smokestack) and the Animal Pathology Building (center right). The building to the lower left is a corncrib.

In 1931, the institute decided to add plant pathology to its studies, and the Plant Pathology Building (right foreground) was constructed in 1932. This building was later renamed Sayre Hall after Dr. Daniel Sayre, the first director of the James Forrestal Research Center. Ultimately, 15 buildings were constructed and another 24 houses provided homes for the staff members and their families. The power plant and Animal Pathology Building are seen in the lower left foreground. (Courtesy of Don Dustin.)

The institute was responsible for many medical advances, including the discovery of the essential nature of viruses. In 1951, the institute moved its laboratory to Rockefeller University in New York City and sold the campus to Princeton University. This view shows the institute *c.* 1935 with its various laboratories, animal pens, and pastures. The small round building on the left is the rabbit hutch. The large buildings are, from left to right, the power plant, the Animal Pathology Building, and the Plant Pathology Building. (Courtesy of Joseph Byrne.)

Over time, Princeton University bought, sold, or developed portions of the land acquired from the institute for varied purposes. As a result, many of the houses and buildings that were part of the Rockefeller Institute for Medical Research were torn down. The only surviving dwelling from the institute is the Theobald Smith House, built for the institute's first director and today used as the community house for Princeton Landing. This photograph was taken c. 1975.

Daniel C. Sayre (1903–1956) was the first director of the James Forrestal Research Center. Sayre Drive is named for him. The center is named for James Forrestal (1892–1949), U.S. secretary of the navy and later the first secretary of defense. He was a Princeton graduate. Here, in December 1958, we see mason Matt Hafenmaier putting the finishing touches on the bust of Forrestal in the center. The bust was later moved to Princeton University. (Courtesy of Matt Hafenmaier.)

95

The James Forrestal Research Center of Princeton University was established in 1951 with the purchase of nine large laboratory buildings and 800 acres of land from the Rockefeller Institute for Medical Research. This relieved the acute research-space problem that the university was experiencing. The university immediately began a construction program for new research, largely funded by federal and industrial grants. The research was fundamental in nature, meaning the "directed but unbounded study of natural phenomena." Among the studies were aeronautical engineering and the studies of atomic nuclei and thermonuclear energy (fusion). Shown c. the early 1960s are the accelerator (the C-shaped building, bottom left), Sayre Hall (middle left), the Long Track Building (far right), the Chemical Sciences building (upper left), the Forrestal machine shop and dispensary (right of Chemical Sciences), the jet propulsion laboratory (above the Long Track Building, upper right), and the Plasma Physics Laboratory B (top center). (Courtesy of the Princeton Forrestal Center.)

The history and advances made at the Princeton Plasma Physics Laboratory (PPPL) are too extensive to cover satisfactorily in this book, but some of those dates and discoveries are listed here. This is an aerial view of the laboratory's C-site, located about a mile east of the main Forrestal site and the laboratory's B-site. The story begins in March 1951, when Lyman Spitzer Jr. proposed to the Atomic Energy Commission the construction of a magnetic plasma device to study controlled fusion. The goal was the production of power using thermonuclear fusion of hydrogen. Approval was granted in July on what was called Project Matterhorn. Research began in the old Rockefeller Research Institute's rabbit hutch. In 1953, the Model A Stellarator was produced. Four years later, the improved B-65 Stellarator was unveiled. An international effort at producing peaceful uses of atomic energy began in 1958, when the controlled thermonuclear research was declassified. In 1960, the C-site was constructed, and in 1961, the name Princeton Plasma Physics Laboratory was adopted. The Model C Stellarator was produced one year later. In July 1969, work was started to convert the Stellarator Model C to a Model C Tokamak, and experiments began in earnest in 1970. These experiments were successful, leading to increased research. Over the next 30 years, the laboratory made many advances and broke several records. The C-site was expanded. In 1974, Congress approved the creation of the Tokamak Fusion Test Reactor to confirm the scientific feasibility of fusion power. Experiments began in December 1975. The first plasma was produced on December 24, 1982. By 1995, the highest temperature ever reached in a laboratory was recorded (510 million degrees Celsius). Today, the laboratory employs almost 500 people on its 72-acre campus, not including graduate students and visiting research staff. It remains at the leading edge of fusion technology and research. (Courtesy of the Princeton Plasma Physics Laboratory.)

The Model C Stellarator began operation in March 1962 and continued in use until July 1969. It was used for the intense study of plasma transport. The C-site was built to house the Model C. (Courtesy of the Princeton Plasma Physics Laboratory.)

Shown here is the interior of the Tokamak Fusion Test Reactor vacuum vessel. The reactor operated from 1982 to 1997 and set several records for the creation of heat. (Courtesy of the Princeton Plasma Physics Laboratory.)

Funded largely by the Atomic Energy Commission and managed jointly by the University of Pennsylvania and Princeton University, the Princeton-Pennsylvania Accelerator building was completed in the early 1960s. By directing a stream of high-energy protons at a substance such as beryllium, a spray of mesons was produced. These mesons were then used to study their nuclear properties. (Courtesy of the Princeton Forrestal Center.)

In February 1957, a nuclear test reactor was built just east of the railroad bridge at Schalks Crossing Road. Constructed by the Industrial Nuclear Reactor Laboratories, a consortium of major companies, the conical dome is 87 feet high and made of 18-inch-thick concrete clad in aluminum. It housed a laboratory for low-level atomic research. The reactor became obsolete and was decontaminated, and ownership reverted to the Walker-Gordon Laboratory Company. Today, it houses the offices of Walker-Gordon and the laboratories of Jacobus Pharmaceuticals.

The Department of Aeronautical Engineering at the James Forrestal Research Center was the university's only teaching department headquartered there. The center housed a gas dynamics laboratory, subsonics laboratory, flight mechanics laboratory, and jet propulsion laboratory. Among their experiments were hovercraft (probably conducted at the flight mechanics laboratory). This photograph shows the P-GEM X-3B. Built in 1960, it had a 180-horsepower engine, weighed 1,240 pounds, flew 24 to 30 inches off the ground, and had a maximum speed of 27 miles per hour. (Courtesy of Barry Nixon.)

Is this the time machine from *Back to the Future*? Well, it is not a DeLorean, but it is a Curtiss-Wright. Experiments on hovercraft—known as air cushion vehicles (ACVs) or ground effect machines (GEMs)—were conducted from the early 1950s until the late 1970s. The chief test pilot was Barry Nixon. By the early 1980s, the facility was shut down. (Courtesy of Barry Nixon.)

The Geophysical Fluid Dynamics Laboratory, formed in 1955, moved to Plainsboro in May 1969. Shown here, the facility (on the James Forrestal campus) is an environmental research laboratory of the National Oceanic and Atmospheric Administration. The scientists at the laboratory experiment with computer models of the atmosphere, studying such concepts as the greenhouse effect. The building houses a supercomputer to create these models. This view is dated March 1977. (Courtesy of the Princeton Forrestal Center.)

The first "research industry" to come to Plainsboro was Firmenich. Founded in Switzerland in 1895, Firmenich (which specializes in fragrances and flavors research) came to New York in 1947. In 1955, it constructed a facility in Plainsboro. Located on Plainsboro Road, just west of the Walker-Gordon Pond, Firmenich eventually acquired 50 acres of Walker-Gordon land. Firmenich is the largest private company in the fragrance and flavor industry in the world. (Courtesy of Firmenich.)

FMC constructed a research-and-development facility in Plainsboro in 1956. The original buildings, shown here, are located on the east side of Route 1, north of Plainsboro Road on the land once called Wellnitz Hill. The company produces chemical products that range in scope from increasing crop yield to making a better detergent. Route 1 is in the foreground of this c. 1956 image. In the upper right is the Ruedemann Farm. (Courtesy of FMC.)

When it arrived and continued to expand, FMC purchased 37 acres of Walker-Gordon land. The company is shown c. 1985 with its many buildings completed. Route 1 is in the foreground, and Plainsboro Road cuts diagonally across the photograph. In the upper left portion of the photograph, Firmenich and part of Walker-Gordon can be seen. To the far lower right is the Holiday Inn, and below that are the Millstone River Apartments. The Hawke-Briggs farmhouse in the lower left is now gone. (Courtesy of FMC.)

102

Eight

WALKER-GORDON AND ELSIE THE COW

Walker-Gordon's story begins in 1891, when Dr. Thomas M. Rotch of Boston concluded that infant deaths could be greatly reduced with careful prescription feeding. He collaborated with Gustavus A. Gordon, a scientist, to develop a modified cow's milk that more closely resembled human milk. George H. Walker, a Boston businessman, became interested in the project and supplied financing. The first laboratory was opened in Boston on December 1, 1891. As a laboratory, Walker-Gordon endeavored to produce sterile milk formulas, following doctors' prescriptions under pristine conditions. However, since there were no milk standards at that time, they soon learned that the final product was very dependent on the initial milk procured. Shown in a photograph from the summer of 1911 are members of the Walker-Gordon Laboratory Company Advisory Committee. They are, from left to right, Henry W. Jeffers Sr. (Plainsboro Farms), C.H. Walker, F.W. Howe, G.W. Franklin, E.C. Hodsdon, and George H. Walker (president). (Courtesy of Glenn Fowler.)

Walker-Gordon's innovative methods were soon the basis for new industry standards. In 1893, the company opened a laboratory in New York City. The milk for the Boston and New York laboratories was purchased from the highest-quality dairies that could be found. Even so, the quality varied enough that the best results could not be achieved. Walker-Gordon thereby concluded that it must have its own dairy farm. In 1897, it purchased 40 acres of farmland in Plainsboro. The town was ideally situated between New York and Philadelphia and had easy access to transportation. The innovative farm would be equipped with a laboratory, medical supervision, and sterilized milking apparatus. In April 1898, Walker-Gordon hired Henry W. Jeffers Sr. to become the resident manager, and the dairy opened that year with 35 cows. Over the next several years, Walker-Gordon began to construct barns, housing, and other buildings. Surplus profits were used to add to the stock and land holdings. Another 256 acres were purchased, and a new milk building was constructed. (By 1929, the farm would have 2,300 acres.) All aspects of production were conducted under the most stringent standards. New cows were kept in quarantine until checked, and all cows were examined every two weeks by the veterinarian. Clean shavings for bedding were used each day. The cows were groomed twice a day. All employees were examined twice a month by a doctor, and the milkers wore sterilized, white overall suits. Additionally, sterile methods of milking were used that included washing, testing, and recording. The milk was also tested in the laboratory for bacterial counts. This photograph is titled "1897—the Beginning—35 Cows!" (Courtesy of Emily Ruedemann.)

Initially, all milking was done by hand. Walker-Gordon, in an attempt to reduce costs and put more money back into the acquisition of stock and land, hired milkers from European countries. Each cow was milked twice a day (later increased to three times), and each man was responsible for milking 30 cows. Walker-Gordon produced a grade classification of milk called Certified Milk, the highest grade possible to obtain. This photograph is dated 1898. Henry Jeffers Sr. is standing to the far right. (Courtesy of the Ruedemann family.)

Before milking, each cow had its udder thoroughly washed and dried. The first milk drawn off was inspected and discarded. Each cow's milk was weighed, recorded, and placed in a sterilized can. It was then taken from the cow buildings to the milk building to be cooled and bottled. The bottles were sealed, packed in ice, and shipped on express trains twice a day. This photograph was taken in a cow barn prior to 1930. (Courtesy of the Jeffers family.)

To carry out all of the dairy functions, Walker-Gordon required many buildings. These buildings were added over time as required. This c. 1906 photograph shows the milk building on the right. It was here that the cooling and bottling took place. Notice the cow weathervane on the cupola. The building in the center left is the powerhouse. The small building to the far left is probably the first office. (Courtesy of the Ruedemann family.)

On the left in this 1913 postcard photograph is the main office. Originally the Ivy Eating Club of Princeton University, it was built in 1889 and moved to Walker-Gordon c. 1910. Next to that is the boardinghouse. Both buildings were torn down in the 1970s. The building on the far right is probably the quarantine barn. This building was used to house new cows to make certain they were healthy before they were mixed with the herd. (Courtesy of Robert Yuell.)

This photograph shows the boardinghouse. Also known as "the clubhouse," this building housed the single men who worked at Walker-Gordon. Built in 1918, it was used up until the time Walker-Gordon ceased production. The building housed a reading room called Woodward Hall. It also contained a dining hall for the men and was open to the public for Sunday meals. Many Plainsboro organizations met in the boardinghouse over the years. The managers were Clara Ridgeway and Lynda Ryan. (Courtesy of Jennie Belle Clark.)

The cows were housed in the barns shown in the background. Each barn held 50 cows. Eventually, there were 33 such barns in use at Walker-Gordon housing 1,650 cows. The barns were connected so that the cows could be easily moved to the milking facility. The fences in front of the barns in this c. 1930s view are exercise pens for the cows. (Courtesy of the Jeffers family.)

Feeding 1,600 cows required 22 million pounds of food annually, primarily alfalfa and corn silage. To hold the silage, Walker-Gordon constructed four concrete silos in 1929. Each silo was approximately 72 feet high and 40 feet in diameter and could hold 3,000 tons of corn silage. These were the largest silos in the world at the time. They were torn down in April 1997. The sign on the truck says, "C.H. Menard Penns Neck, NJ." (Courtesy of the Jeffers family.)

Here we see the process of storing the silage as it was originally performed. The horse- or truck-drawn wagons bring the stalks up to the chopper (seen behind the old truck). The stalks are then loaded inside the chopper, cut into small pieces, and then blown through pipes from the chopper to the top of the pile. (Courtesy of the Jeffers family.)

Eventually, it proved faster and more economical to store the silage in trenches dug and lined with sheeting. The silage was cut, dumped into the trench, and covered with tarps. These became the largest trench silos in the world. To the left are the original food storage silos that were housed near the barns. The large silos shown earlier, no longer needed for silage, were used instead to house peanut shells. Peanut shells were used for cow bedding. This photograph dates from c. late 1940. The truck lettering reads, "L.A. Clarke, Plainsboro, NJ." (Courtesy of the Jeffers family.)

Walker-Gordon made a precise study of the effects of a cow's nutritional needs and the effect on her milk. They discovered, for example, that dehydrated alfalfa provided seven times more vitamin A than sun-dried alfalfa. Each cow was provided with a precise, balanced ration. The ration consisted of corn silage, alfalfa, grass silage, barley, oats, cornmeal, and several other grains and foodstuffs. In this c. 1930s view, an unidentified man forks feed into the troughs from the feed trays. (Courtesy of the Jeffers family.)

Originally, Walker-Gordon owned its cows. Then, in 1939, the operation decentralized. The cows were now owned by "cow unit operators." Each unit consisted of 50 cows. The unit operators kept their lactating cows in the Walker-Gordon barns but kept their dry stock and young cows at their own rented farm. Walker-Gordon milked the cows and provided barn space and feed. The unit operator was responsible for the cow's care and was paid on the amount and quality of milk produced by their cows. This photograph is dated May 29, 1939. (Courtesy of the Jeffers family.)

Only cows that have recently birthed calves can provide milk. Therefore, until artificial insemination was used, more than 75 purebred bulls were housed at the Walker-Gordon Farm. They are seen here in their bull barn. Cows not lactating were called "dry stock" and were maintained at separate farms by the unit operators. (Courtesy of the Jeffers family.)

110

At first, Walker-Gordon produced and raised its own cows. When the pregnant cow was near delivery, it was moved to a maternity ward. Once the calf was born, it was taken to one of the three on-site calf barns, where it was carefully raised under scientific conditions and rations. In 1939, Walker-Gordon began to decentralize this process and calves were raised at surrounding farms, many of them outside New Jersey. (Courtesy of the Jeffers family.)

Veterinarians were on duty at the Walker-Gordon Farm 24 hours a day. The cows received a health checkup daily and, each month, would be given a thorough medical exam. Each cow had a health record and milk record card. Sick cows were sent to the quarantine barn, where they were treated until fully recovered. The people who worked with the cows were also required to have regular medical checkups provided by the Walker-Gordon physician. In this view, Dr. Gustave Kimnach examines a cow. (Courtesy of the Jeffers family.)

Special feed, medical supervision, extraordinary sanitary conditions, and express delivery all resulted in increased costs. To produce milk at reasonable costs, a less labor-intensive milking method was required. Henry Jeffers Sr. came up with a solution—the Rotolactor. The Rotolactor was a type of cow "merry-go-round." Cows would be led onto the machine, hooked up to a milking device, and milked in one revolution. When the revolution was completed, the cow would be led off the platform. Jeffers had conceived the idea in 1913 on a trip to Europe. When he returned, plans were drawn up by George Fisher, and initial designs and experiments started, but World War I brought them to a halt. In 1928, the idea was resurrected. The board of directors approved the $200,000 adventure, and in 1928, construction began. The Rotolactor created much interest. In 1929, the Borden Company bought the stock of the Walker-Gordon Laboratory Company. This provided the necessary resources for the project. On November 13, 1930, the secretary of agriculture, Arthur Hyde and the governor of New Jersey, Morgan Larson, came to Plainsboro for the unveiling. Thomas Edison had been invited to attend the ceremonies and to start the machine, but unfortunately, he was too ill. Instead, he pushed a telegraph key from the library in his Menlo Park home that started the Rotolactor. From the beginning, the Rotolactor was an unqualified success. It created a system where milk went from the cow to the bottle with virtually no exposure to the air or contamination. The Rotolactor could hold 50 cows and milk about 250 cows an hour. Initially, the cows were milked three times a day. This was changed to twice a day in early 1951. At its height, the Rotolactor milked some 1,650 cows a day and produced 26,000 quarts of milk daily. This photograph of the Rotolactor shows a group of children with their teachers and bus driver, watching the Rotolactor in operation. They are standing in the visitor's observation room in the Rotolactor building. The man in the center bottom of the photograph is Ed Campbell. (Courtesy of the Jeffers family.)

112

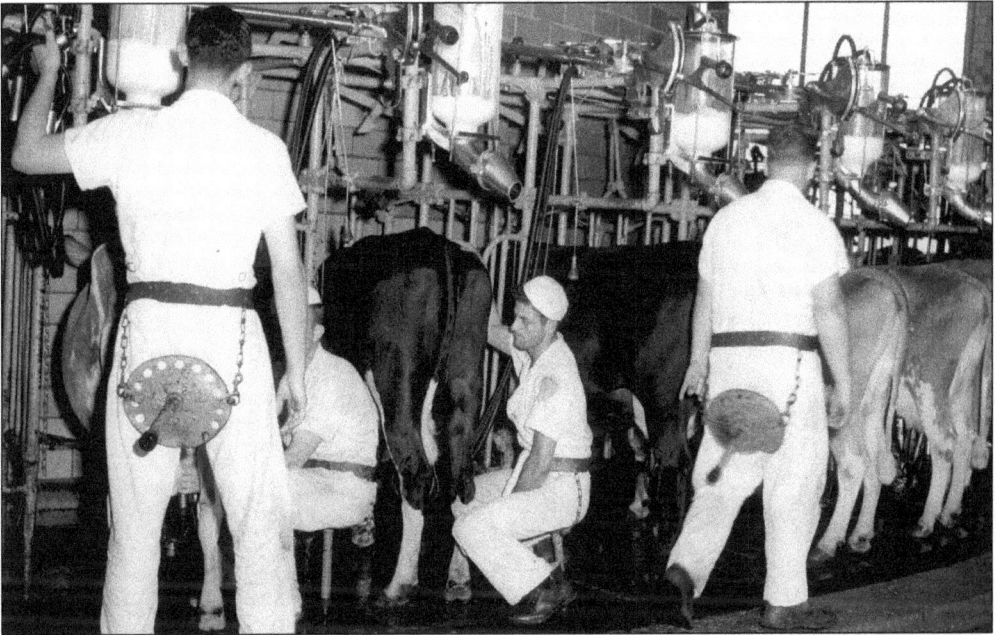

The cow entered the Rotolactor building and was washed with warm water. As she stepped aboard the Rotolactor, a stanchion closed around her neck to hold her in place. Her udder was then dried with a sterilized towel and inspected, after which milk was taken from each udder and examined. The cow was then attached to the milking machine. As she rode around the Rotolactor, her milk was drawn into a Pyrex jar above her station. This photograph dates from July 14, 1954. (Courtesy of the Jeffers family.)

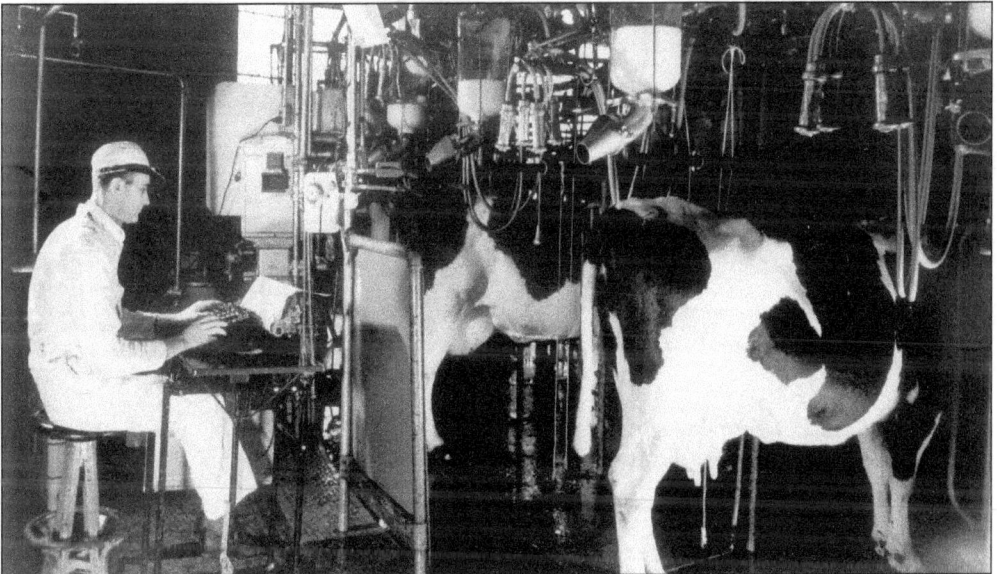

The teat cups were then removed. The milk automatically flowed into a weighing device and was recorded, as shown here. The milk then flowed to the processing and bottling room, and the automatic milking system was sterilized for the next cow. When the stanchion opened, the cow stepped off the Rotolactor and returned to her barn to be fed. The milking process took about 12 minutes. (Courtesy of the Jeffers family.)

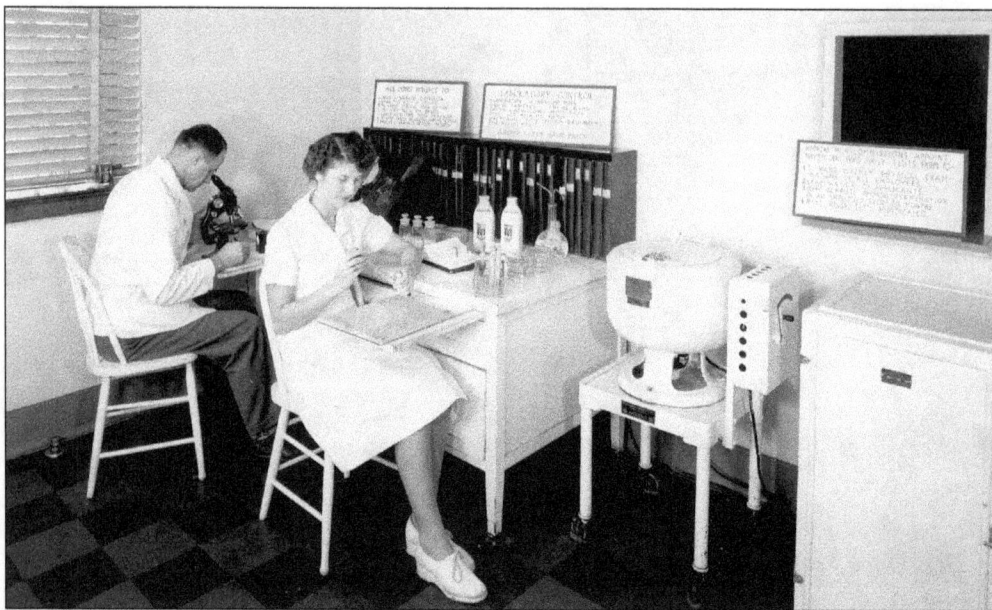

Technicians at Walker-Gordon inspected the milk daily in the control laboratory for bacteria content, purity, and quality. In addition, Walker-Gordon continued to test for and develop new products. Eventually, they produced certified raw milk, certified pasteurized milk, certified skimmed milk, protein milk, lactic milk, and acidophilus milk. In this view, John Bryan and Eleanor Cannon conduct tests in the laboratory. (Courtesy of the Jeffers family.)

The Rotolactor was housed in this building. Over the visitor's entrance was a brass plaque of Henry Jeffers Sr. (barely visible in this c. 1930 photograph), which was designed by Hermann Carl Mueller. The Rotolactor contained the records room, laboratories, and offices. It was nicknamed the "round barn" by employees and also used by the community. During World War II, the roof was raised to aid in spotting enemy planes. (Courtesy of the Jeffers family.)

In 1929, Henry Jeffers Sr. commissioned the Mueller Mosaic Company of Trenton, founded by Herman Carl Mueller, to create 15 colored-tile panels that depicted the history of bovine agriculture. The murals circled the upper portion of the visitor's observation room. Each mural was 30 inches high and 96 inches long and was separated from the other by a tiled Walker-Gordon crest. Mueller also crafted a half-scale Jersey cow head used as a water fountain in the observation area. (Courtesy of the Jeffers family.)

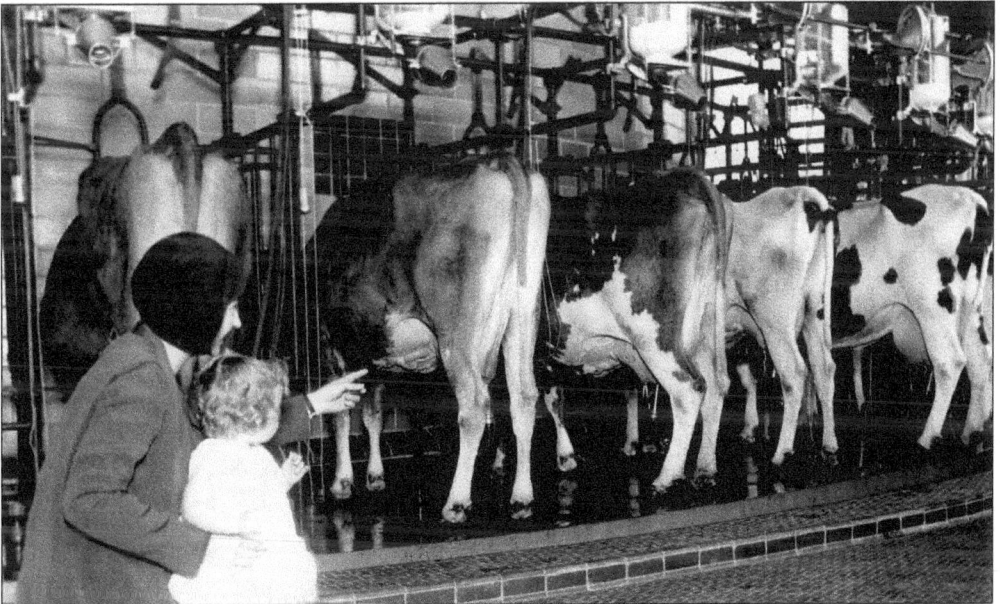

The Rotolactor and Walker-Gordon were visited by 200,000 people a year. Schoolchildren came by the busload to visit the farm and learn about the dairy industry. In the visitor's observation room, a small circular area sold ice-cream and dairy products. Visitors were supplied with material to take a self-guided tour of the sites. Shown c. 1933 are two Plainsboro residents visiting the Rotolactor—Mrs. Robert Knight and her daughter Priscilla (Knight) Stitt. (Courtesy of the Jeffers family.)

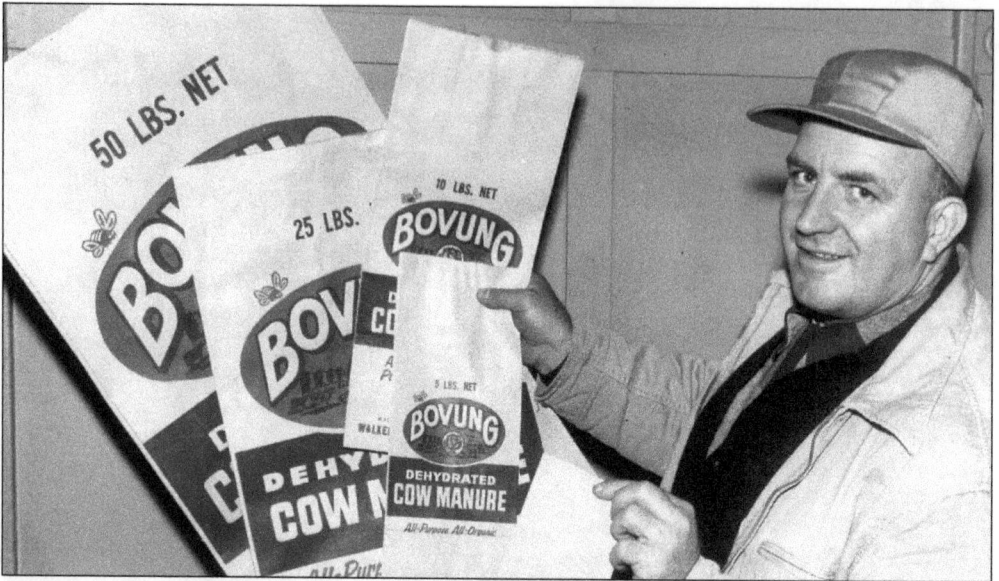

The manure from the cows belonged to Walker-Gordon, not to the cow unit operators, and Walker-Gordon put it to good use. Bovung (dehydrated cow manure), Bovette (deodorized Bovung for indoor plants), and Bovert (lawn and garden fertilizer) were all profitable products. The manure was dehydrated in the winter in the same machine used to dehydrate the alfalfa in the summer. In this photograph, Chester Sheen, vice president and production supervisor, displays the Bovung bag sizes. (Courtesy of Chet Steen.)

Walker-Gordon products were shipped by train initially and later by truck. Before trucks were refrigerated, the milk was packed in ice and the truck bodies were insulated. Local deliveries were made by truck to the doorstep every day. This unrefrigerated Walker-Gordon truck was owned by John K. Holohan, who was also the town's justice of the peace. The license plate date on this Brockway truck is 1930. (Courtesy of the Jeffers family.)

Prior to 1939, Elsie the Cow was a popular advertising caricature for the Borden Company. At the 1939 New York World's Fair, the Borden exhibit housed a miniature 10-stanchion Rotolactor. The Rotolactor milked 150 cows each day. At the exhibit, the young Borden hostesses fielded questions. Sixty percent of the visitors asked, "Which of the cows is Elsie?" Having no answer, Borden quickly selected a cow from Brookfield, Massachusetts, named "You'll Do Lobelia," shown here, to play the role.

Elsie was an immediate hit. Recognizing her popularity, Borden put her on the Rotolactor to ride alone twice each day. The next year, the company created a special display for the star. Elsie's "Boudoir" was done up in early "Barn Colonial," with churns for tables, milk bottles for lamps, and a wheelbarrow for a chaise lounge. The Borden exhibit became the most popular at the New York World's Fair. When she was not working at the fair or on tour, Elsie's home was the Walker-Gordon Farm in Plainsboro.

In 1940, Elsie was offered an RKO movie contract to play the role of Buttercup in *Little Men*. Borden was concerned. Elsie was pregnant. Also, who would take her place at the fair? RKO promised the best of prenatal care, so Elsie went west and Borden's invented a husband, Elmer, to take Elsie's place. The "Boudoir" became a messy bachelor pad until Elsie returned with baby Beulah. Standing behind Elsie on the set is Chet Steen. (Courtesy of Chet Steen.)

Ultimately, Elsie's numerous personal appearances led to her death. While traveling to the New York theater district in April 1941, she was severely injured in a truck accident in Rahway. She was rushed back to Plainsboro, but her injuries proved too serious, and she had to be euthanized. Elsie was buried at the Walker-Gordon Farm. Her marker, shown here, has been moved several times but still remains close to her final resting place. (Photograph by Bill Hart.)

When they were not traveling, Elsie, Elmer, and Beulah lived in the calf barns at Walker-Gordon. In December 1944, Henry Jeffers Sr. and some associates purchased Walker-Gordon back from Borden, causing Elsie to move elsewhere. Shown here with Elsie at Wrigley Field in July 1944 are Anna (left) and Edith Perrine. Anna and Edith were from West Windsor and cared for Elsie on her national travels for four years. Here they are auctioning off a calf to raise money for war bonds.

The Walker-Gordon Gate House restaurant was located on the southeast corner of Route 1 and Plainsboro Road. A delightful dining experience, it specialized in fried chicken, steaks, and homemade pies. Vegetables used in the restaurant were grown in a garden behind the establishment. Built in 1934, it had three dining rooms and a capacity of 75 people. The restaurant closed c. 1952 and was torn down c. 1962. H.E. "Buck" Watlington was the chef from 1934 to 1940.

In this *c.* 1940 photograph, the Pennsylvania Railroad runs from the upper left to the middle right. Plainsboro Road crosses from the center left to the upper right. By the 1960s, shortages in farm labor and price wars in the milk industry were driving costs up and profits down at Walker-Gordon. On June 18, 1971, the Rotolactor milked its last cow, and Walker-Gordon dairy functions ceased. Over several years, the buildings were demolished, the silos coming down in 1997. Today, the farm is home to the Walker Gordon Farms housing development.

The Walker-Gordon Rotolactor milking crew appears in a photograph captioned, "Last Day of Milking—6/18/1971." From left to right are the following: (front row) Earl Holland, Bob Allison, Ken Robbins, Harold (Stubby) Lovell, Stan Hettinger, Wyatt Fenity, and Milton (Shinny) Shinn; (back row) Henry Jeffers III, Robert Bidenbauch, Herman (Romeo) Barksdale, Chester Steen, Frank (Buss) Powell, and George (Pogy) Noble.

Nine

PARTING SHOTS

The intense development of the last 30 years has changed Plainsboro from a sleepy farm village to a busy suburban town. The farms' greatest cash crop turned out to be housing, and the population has increased more than tenfold. This aerial view was taken in the late 1940s, before the development began. Plainsboro Road starts in the lower left and angles to the upper right. Edgemere Avenue runs from the bottom right until it crosses Plainsboro Road and becomes Dey Road. You can just make out the Plainsboro Hotel on the corner. In the center of the picture, the Wicoff School is plainly visible. To its left is the First Presbyterian Church. Directly across the street from the church is the old Mechanics Hall. The street running alongside Mechanics Hall is Schalks Crossing Road. The house to the left is where the Plainsboro Shopping Center stands today.

Plainsboro's link to the Colonial period is represented by the Flemer House, located on Mapleton Road north of St. Joseph's. The house was built in 1756 by Matthias Van Dyke on a 200-acre piece of land he inherited from his father. British officers were occupying the house just before the Battle of Princeton, and a British cannonball struck the house during a skirmish. The house is built of irregularly cut fieldstone and passed through several owners before William Flemer. (Courtesy of Bill Flemer III.)

Dr. Guy Dean Jr., Plainsboro's first resident physician, came to Princeton Hospital as a resident in 1937. In 1940, he set up an office in Plainsboro at 503 Plainsboro Road, where he practiced for 25 years. During those years, he served not only the hospital and township but also Walker-Gordon. Shown on his office and residence steps are, from left to right, the following: (front row) John Freed (Dr. Dean's father-in-law) and Dr. Dean; (back row) Cora Freed (Dr. Dean's stepmother-in-law), Marion Freed Dean (Dr. Dean's wife), and Mary Freed (Marion's half-sister). (Courtesy of Guy Dean III.)

No farm town would be complete without a 4-H club. This is the Plainsboro Pals, a girl's 4-H club. The group was led by Helen Pendyke and Doris Parker. Pictured *c.* 1950 are, from left to right, Judy Parker, Ann Wicoff, Linda Pendyke, Carla Eiker, Vivian Hullfish, Joan Pendyke, Florence Losey, Donna Pendyke, Lucille Hullfish, and Phyllis Parker. (Courtesy of Donna Pendyke.)

Between school, farm chores, and club meetings, Plainsboro's children found time for parties and play. This photograph was taken on July 5, 1941, behind the two-room schoolhouse. The First Presbyterian manse is on the left; the school is on the right. From left to right are Priscilla (Knight) Stitt, Rudy Wellnitz, Bill Murphy, Leonard Luther, Pat (Hamlet) Runko, Charles Krukowski, Wesley Holman, and Della (Stout) Nemes. (Courtesy of Priscilla Stitt and Della Nemes.)

123

The adults played when they could, too. This photograph shows the Plainsboro Gunning Club, started in the 1930s as a Walker-Gordon organization. Its membership was extended to the township in the mid-1950s. The group owned an old Plainsboro train station toolshed (shown here) that was moved to a site across from the recycling center. The club is still active. From left to right are Jimmy Christerson, Bill Bennet, Dave Nitchman, George Grant, and Bud Byrnes. (Courtesy of Charlie Miller.)

Migrant farm workers were a big part of Plainsboro life. Their annual appearance was crucial to the success of a labor-intensive harvest. The migrant farm children attended the local schools, and their parents shopped in the local shops, which each year stocked up for the increased population. This photograph of two migrant farm worker children was taken in the early 1940s on the Joseph Magnani Farm. (Courtesy of the Joseph Magnani family.)

Today, Plainsboro is a suburban town filled with community developments and industrial parks. This photograph shows the Princeton Forrestal campus, which encompasses much of the old Rockefeller Institute for Medical Research. Route 1 is in the foreground. In the upper left are Schalks Crossing Road and the Princeton Collection. College Road East winds on the right, and Research Way connects College Road East to Schalks Crossing Road. (Courtesy of the Princeton Forrestal Center.)

The Robert Wood Johnson Foundation was created in New Brunswick in 1936 and came to Plainsboro in 1972. It is the largest philanthropy foundation in the United States devoted to healthcare and the largest foundation based in New Jersey. It is shown here in its home on the Princeton Forrestal campus. (Courtesy of the Princeton Forrestal Center.)

Founded on March 15, 1917, in Huntingdon, Pennsylvania, the American Re-Insurance Company came to Plainsboro in 1988. By moving its corporate headquarters from New York to Plainsboro, the company (located on College Road East) saved millions of dollars in rent and taxes. Its symbol is an eagle, visible here in the lower right-hand corner. (Courtesy of the American Re-Insurance Company.)

Merrill Lynch built an office on 275 acres of Plainsboro land in 1985. Located on the south side of Scudders Mill Road, the complex opened up as an international conference and training center and as offices for administrative and support services for both the Asset Management Insurance Group and the Private Client Group. Much like Walker-Gordon 85 years earlier, Merrill Lynch chose Plainsboro in part for its easy access by all modes of transportation. (Courtesy of the Merrill Lynch Archives.)

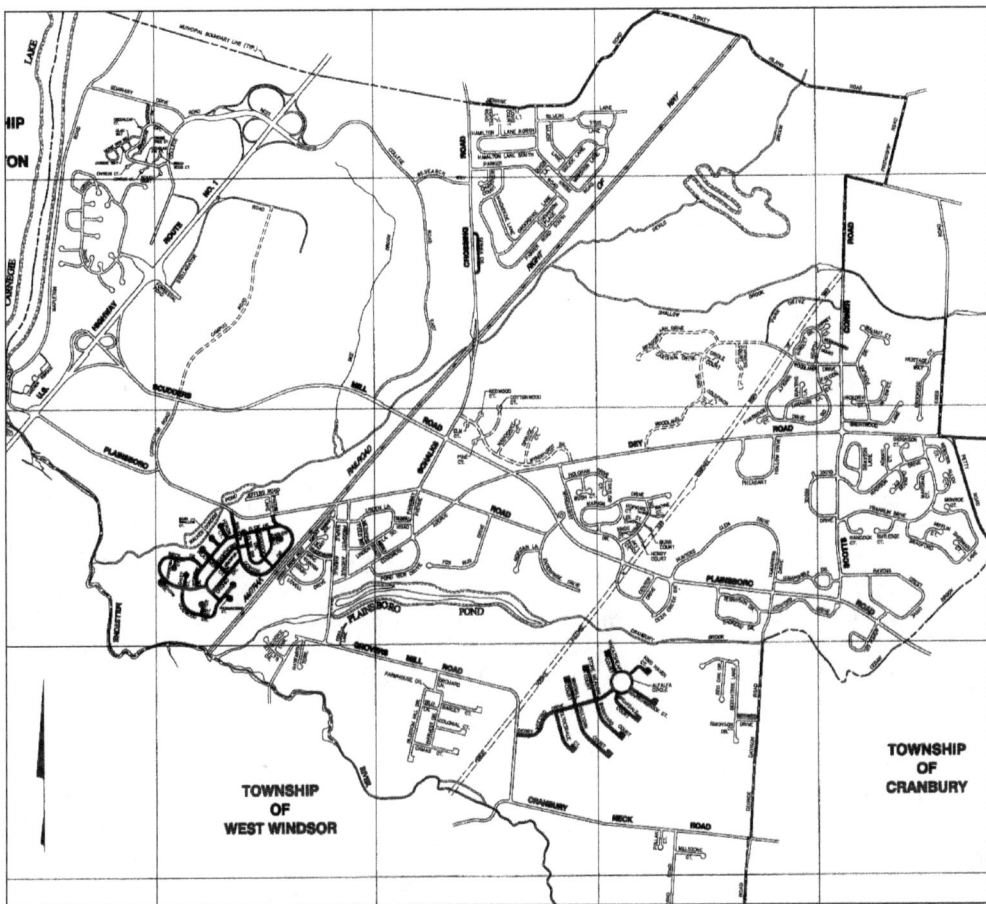

Plainsboro today is the home to more than 20,000 people. This map dates from September 2000. A comparison to the 1939 map shows which farms became which developments. In the upper left (Sayre Drive), Princeton Landing, Princeton Forrestal Village, and Princeton Forrestal campus now occupy the land of Rockefeller Institute for Medical Research. In the lower left by the railroad tracks, the Walker Gordon housing development now resides where the Walker-Gordon Farm once stood. In the upper center (Schalks Crossing Road), the Princeton Collection and Princeton Gallery Estates now stand where the Parkers once raised chickens. Below that, Serina Drive and the Plainsboro Acres occupy the W. Dennison Farm. Lower still, Wyndhurst Drive and the Winder Grove and Princeton Crossing developments sit on the old Wicoff Farm. Fox Run Apartments and Enterprise Drive Businesses occupy the Britton Farm. So do the Villas at Cranbury Brook, just east of Fox Run. In the lower right, the Brittany and Hampshire now sit on the Davison Farm. To the left of that, at Derry Meeting Drive, the Crossing at Grovers Mill Estates stands on Walker-Gordon property that was once farmed by the Bolles and Wellnitz family. To the far right, north of Dey Road and east of Scotts Corner Road, is Shallowbrook and Brentwood Estates, which was once the Petty Farm. Farther west, off Dey Road on Woodland Drive, the Estates at Plainsboro sit on the Henry Jeffers and Frank Katona Farms. Princeton Manor, off Woodland Drive, occupies the E.S. Barclay and Pierri Farms. South of Dey Road and east of Scotts Corner Road is the Gentry, which was the Simonson and Anderson Farms. Finally, Ravens Crest and Aspen occupy the Mason Farm, while the Hunters Glen Apartments and the golf course are on the Mount and Nathaniel Britton Farms. This map was prepared by David J. Samuel, township engineer, in conjunction with CME Associates, Consulting and Municipal Engineers.

127

BIBLIOGRAPHY

A Description of the Walker-Gordon System of Agriculture As Developed in Producing a New Milk. Author, publisher, and date unknown.

A New, More Vital Milk and the Factors in Its Production. Author, publisher, and date unknown.

Anniversary 1914/1989 St. Joseph's Preparatory Seminary. Author and publisher unknown. 1989.

Cushman, Helen Baker. *The Church at the Crossroad: A History of Princeton Alliance Church.* Westfield, New Jersey: Ministry Press, 1999.

Fenity, Leo W. *Walker-Gordon: Parts I, II, III, and IV.* 1991.

Simmons, Uriel J., Editor. *Gotham Herdsman 1939 New York World's Fair.* Publisher and date unknown.

Steen, Ruth Carriker. *The Steen Family in Plainsboro 1947–1982.* Publisher and date unknown.

The James Forrestal Research Center Princeton University. Author, publisher, and date unknown.

Walker-Gordon Milk All Large Cities. Author, publisher, and date unknown.

Walker-Gordon Milk Bulletin. Vol. 1. May 1921–April 1922. Walker-Gordon Laboratory Company.

Tindall, Edward E., M.S., D.V.M., and C. Stanton Clark. *Walker-Gordon: One of a Kind.* Stockton, New Jersey: Covered Bridge Press, 1998.

www.ingramcontent.com/pod-product-compliance
Lightning Source LLC
Chambersburg PA
CBHW050656150426
42813CB00055B/2197